# FIFTY YEARS AS A JOURNALIST

**Mulk Raj Saraf**

INDIA • SINGAPORE • MALAYSIA

ISBN 979-8-89610-266-3

# Contents

Contents

# Jamna Devi Gian Devi Saraf Trust

## Promoting Conscientious Journalism

The Jamna Devi Gian Devi Saraf Trust, briefly known as the JDGD Saraf Trust, was established on August 9, 1985, by Lala Mulk Raj Saraf, widely regarded as the "Father of Journalism" in Jammu and Kashmir, along with his eldest son, Mr. Om Prakash Saraf, an eminent journalist in his own right. The Trust was named in honour of their respective mothers, Jamna Devi and Gian Devi. Today, it is managed by Mrs. Rachna Vinod and Dr. Sonali Gupta, granddaughter and great-granddaughter of Lala Mulk Raj Saraf.

The JDGD Saraf Trust is honoured to republish Lala Mulk Raj Saraf's autobiography, "Fifty Years as a Journalist," to commemorate 100 years of journalism in Jammu and Kashmir. The first edition of the book was originally published in 1967.

Fifty Years as a Journalist

First Edition: May 1967

Reprint Edition: June 2024

Published By:

Jamna Devi Gian Devi Saraf Trust

Jammu

www.jdgdsaraftrust.org

Contact: 7780947446

Email: jdgdsaraftrust@gmail.com

ISBN:

Price:

*A saga in journalism dating back to the times when applying for permission to bring out a newspaper was looked upon as an act against the State.*

# Introduction

Lala Mulk Raj Saraf is the pioneer of journalism in Jammu and Kashmir and Founder-Editor of the Ranbir, which was the first newspaper in this State. After a long and rich career he has put down his reminiscences covering people and events over the last half century. A great deal has happened in this State during this period, and it is very interesting to this panoramic vision through the eyes of Shri Saraf. His book throws interesting light upon many facets of contemporary history and I commend the veteran journalist on his Autobiography.

Karan Singh
Governor
Hari Niwas
Jammu
March 9, 1967

# Foreword

Journalism has been aptly described as the Fourth Estate, and its great importance in any present-day society can hardly be overemphasised, more so, in a country like ours where a vast programme of social reconstruction is under way. It is, therefore, in the fitness of things that Lala Mulk Raj Saraf, who is popularly known as the father of journalism in Jammu and Kashmir, should have recorded his valuable experience in the field.

Lala Mulk Raj Saraf has not only been pioneer in the field of journalism, but also a distinguished publicman, and has always maintained a high standard of behaviour.

I have enjoyed reading his reminiscences immensely, and I am sure that this account will not only be of benefit to young and aspiring journalists, but will also interest all those who have a stake in a clean and purposeful life.

I may add that the book deals with an important period in the history of Jammu and Kasmir State, and will as such constitute a valuable source of information and reference for serious students of contemporary history.

G.M. Sadiq
Chief Minister
Jammu and Kashmir State
Jammu Tawi
April 5, 1967

# Preface

Right from the year 1920 onward, the State of Jammu and Kashmir has passed through many a vicissitude. From autocracy it has been transformed into a democracy as an integral part of the largest democracy in the world. It has been my proud privilege to be an eye-witness to, if not an active participant in, all this great change. Not only this, I have had also the honour of contributing my humble bit in the development of what has come to be known as the Fourth Estate of the Realm.

It is now nearly five decades that I have been experimenting with journalism in Jammu and Kashmir. In the pages that follow, I have made an attempt to narrate my victories as also to indicate my setbacks in my fight for journalism.

If the study of my trials and turmoil, successes and failures, as embodied in this book may enable a journalist to discover himself even to a slight degree and lead him on to the road –

*Through long and dreary*
*To foot it bravely, strong and weary*

I would consider my labour amply rewarded.

The present volume is only a part of a bigger work, A LOOK AT THE LAST FIFTY YEARS, which may take some more time to complete.

In the preparation of the book, I have been ably assisted by my sons Om, Suraj and Prem. From start to finish they spared no pains to see the book through.

The Governor Dr. Karan Singh (now Union Minister for Tourism and Civil Aviation) has very kindly written the Introduction. I am grateful to the Chief Minister, Khwaja Ghulam Mohammad Sadiq for going through the manuscript and writing the Foreword.

The messages sent by the Acting Governor M. Janaki Nath Wazir (Chief Justice) and Shri M.A. Ansari, formerly Chief Justice, Kerala High Court and Chairman Anti-Corruption Commission J&K State are thankfully acknowledged.

A word more. Like most journalists and pressmen, I have also had my share of suffering but how much sufferings-physical, mental and financial that saintly woman, my partner in life, Shrimati Gian Devi, has undergone because of me, would never be known. I would not have been what I am today, without her.

Mulk Raj Saraf
Jammu May 1, 1967

# CHAPTER 1

## Early Years

I was born on April 8, 1894 at Samba in Jammu District.

In the first decade of my life, I cannot find any spectacular factors which might have been shadows of coming events. My grandfather, Shri Kalu Shah, was a jeweller. On account of his avocation our family came to be surnamed as Saraf. My father, Shri Daya Ram Saraf, however ran a drapery and merchandise establishment. We were five brothers. At the turn of the present century plague epidemic played havoc with our family: my father and two elder brothers, Shri Faqir Chand and Shri Khushi Ram, were no more. Shortly afterwards, my mother, Shrimati Jamna Devi, too, took to her heavenly abode. She came from a respectable family of Zafarwal in Sialkot District (now in Pakistan). Two years later my younger brother Ganda Mal also passed away. My elder brother Shri Karam Chand Saraf and myself were the only survivors of the family. He was then eleven years of age, I two years younger. He died in March 1964 at the age of 72.

We were looked after by our uncle Shri Mangu Shah. He opened a small shop for my elder brother, who, from the very start, seemed nimble-witted and clever. On account of domestic handicaps, I could not begin my education early, therefore I tried to sit on the shop. My inclination, however, was averse to shopkeeping. Time and again, I crammed Dogri letters and Mahajan arithmetic but every time they soon eluded my memory.

In that hopeless milieu, I became eleven years old. An ordinary event at this juncture completely changed the course of my life. In 1905, the Prince of Wales, who afterwards became the King George V of the United Kingdom, came on a trip to India and also visited Jammu. In his honour numerous functions were arranged including distribution of sweets etcetera in Educational Institutions. Perhaps, attracted by that, I joined the local school.

Having started my education at a comparatively advanced age, I had many advantages, both physical and mental. I was respected by my classmates. I was also an obedient pupil. Once I carried quite ungrudgingly a load of over a mound of vegetables on my head straight from Jammu to Samba, a distance of 25 miles which I had to cover on foot (in absence of any vehicular traffic there in those days) in consecutive two days simply because I had been asked by my school teachers to bring for each of them fresh vegetables from the capital city, of course, in lieu of cash price paid in advance by them. Rather, I felt proud and content, within myself for having accomplished the task for allotment of which, out of all the students, I alone had, as I rightly claimed, the privilege and the pleasure to be singled out.

When I had reached fourth primary class, my uncle gave my elder brother his share from the common family property, My brother, thereupon, migrated to a nearby village. Not unoften, I had to take private tuition or perform odd jobs to meet my expenses for books and clothes. When I passed my fifth class, my uncle tried to get me recruited as a field map measurer in the Land Settlement Department but that was not to be.

In the meantime, I developed a taste for reading newspapers. The father of one of my classmates was a postman. In those days two Lahore Urdu weeklies viz., The Rajput Gazette and the Akbar-i-Aam used to reach Samba. The postman, a Rajput, subscribed for the Rajput Gazette which I used to go through zealously in his house. My penchant for reading newspapers increased to such an extent that I hardly let a day pass without reading one newspaper or the other.

In 1913 I passed my middle school examination. Luckily that very year, high classes were started in Samba and I joined the ninth class. I was awarded a monthly scholarship of rupees four. My elder brother soon re-migrated to Samba where he soon secured a lucrative business. With his increasing prosperity he deeply felt my separation. At last, I left my uncle and entered my ancestral house. My brother felt relieved, and his wife celebrated it as an auspicious occasion.

In 1915, at the age of 21, I passed my matriculation examination. I had already joined as an officiating Laboratory Assistant in the Samba High School at Rs. 12/- per month soon after taking the examination. On account of my poor health, I was reluctant to continue my studies. My brother who was extremely pleased with my success in the annual examination, however, insisted on my joining the College. I obeyed him.

Thus, in the year 1915, I joined the Prince of Wales College, now named the Government Gandhi Memorial College, Jammu. I made full use of the library and reading room there. Having the opportunity to study so many newspapers and magazines, free of cost, I felt immense pleasure and read avidly. Newspaper study soon began to turn into a hobby for journalism. I wrote my first article for the College periodical, Tawi, in 1915.

My interest in the political and social conditions of the State began to develop fast. Once or twice, I wrote for the Kashmiri magazine published from Lahore. The editor and proprietor of that paper was the renowned litterateur, poet and historian, Moulavi Mohd-ud -Din Fauq, with whom I had very contemporaneous connections in the later years.

Once our Professor of History, Shri T.I. Magarmilani, questioned me in the class about my programme in life after leaving the college. I expressed my brame to see four things in the State, viz, a newspaper, a legislative assembly, a university and a bank. By the grace of Almighty, Jammu and Kashmir has since advanced in all these directions and I have the satisfaction of having contributed my bit to all of them in their embryonic stages.

*With his elder brother Shri Karam Chand Saraf to
whom the Author owes so much*

I can never forget an incident in my life which happened towards the end of my college career. Due to the martial law conditions in the Punjab following the fateful days of the Jallianwala Bagh massacre, our centre for the degree examination (1919) had been shifted from Lahore to Sialkot where I was staying with a friend of mine, Shri Ram Rakha Mal Mahajan. I fell sick during the examination days and was much reduced physically. Nevertheless, I continued to sit in the examination, of course, with little hope of success. The Superintendent of the Examination was the Principal of Mission College, Sialkot – a noble Englishman. One day when I had finished with my Economics Paper, I handed it over to the Superintendent as usual. At once a thought struck me that I had made a serious blunder which needed to be rectified. So, I earnestly requested the Superintendent that I want my answer-book back for a few seconds to correct a word or two therein. The Superintendent was kind enough to return it for doing the needful. While going through the paper hurriedly in the presence of the Superintendent and changing a word here and there, I found one whole paragraph erroneous which made my reply to other parts of the same question meaningless. I erased the whole paragraph and handed back the answer-book to him. Returning to my residence, I began to prepare for the Economics Paper B for the next day. But I found myself upset. My peace of mind had gone. The thought weighed heavily upon my mind, nay upon my soul, that beyond correcting a word or two, I had committed a breach of faith and hence a sin by erasing a paragraph without bringing it to the notice of the Superintendent. I tried to console myself by arguing out in my mind in a hundred and one ways but in vain. The thought of having behaved, rather misbehaved in the way I did, haunted me in everything I wanted to do that afternoon. I was unable to pursue my studies anymore and could not properly attend to my illness, the ailment in me seemed to have left me for a while.

At long last, thought flashed across my mind. Why should I not go to the Superintendent and confess my guilt and seek his blessings? The very thought of it smoothened my mind. It was evening time. I straightway went to the Mission College to find out where the Principal (Superintendent) lived. As it was getting dark, I almost ran towards the residence of the principal which was situated in the cantonment area. Due to martial law the whole atmosphere was surcharged with suspicion and fear. An Indian youth strolling in cantonment area – Whiteman's enclave in British Baj – at odd hours? I was actually questioned by a sentry here and a sentry there but I succeeded each time in proving my *bona fides* that as a candidate in the degree examination that was on in the city, I urgently needed to meet the Principal. I was allowed to proceed till I reached the destination. On seeing me there the Principal enquired as to what had brought me there. I related to him the story of my said plight and asked for his pardon. That noble Englishman very humbly yet touchingly observed "Ask His pardon who pardons us all". He did not utter a word more. For a moment I stood motionless and then thought of Him Who pardons us all. And I found the solution to my entire satisfaction then and there. I bowed to the Principal and came back greatly relieved and calmly pursued my work. The next day after I had done my paper, I erased with my pen one whole answer I considered to be the best done and for which I expected the highest marks. Thus I atoned for the Sin which I had committed the previous day. This was actually the solution which had struck me at the time of my meeting with the Principal when he had advised me to "ask His pardon Who pardons us all". Yet another happy paradox was that notwithstanding my early diffidence about my success in the degree examination chiefly due to my failure to do full justice to my question papers on the whole, coupled with my illness during the examination days, I felt not merely overburdened but so completely convinced within myself the moment I destroyed my best answer as a measure of my expiation, that no power on earth henceforth could fail me. I was indeed placed in high second class when degree examination results were announced after two months.

After I had got through my degree examination in 1919, my respected brother again desired that I should proceed on in my studies. He advised me to join the Law College, Lahore. In fact, he wanted to see me as a Judge after my law course. I, however, had no inclination for the law as I had none for shopkeeping. Yet I had to follow the desire of my brother, and it did benefit me ultimately though in a different way.

In the wake of martial law the Punjab had been shaken in its entrails. The top material personalities frequently used to visit Lahore and Amritsar. I considered it my good luck to be so close to the leaders like Mahatma Gandhi, Lokmanya Tilak, Dr Annie Besant, Lala Lajpat Roy, Pandit Moti Lal Nehru, Pandit Madan Mohan Malviya, Dr Ansari, Hakim Ajmal Khan, Swami Shradhanandji Ji, Shri C.R. Das, Babu Bipan Paul, Maulana Azad, Maulana Mohd. Ali, Sardar Patel, Shri Shrinivasa Shastri and Baba Kharak Singh and hear their inspiring ideas. Pandit Jawahar Lal Nehru and Netaji Subhash Chandra Bose were not so renowned then. I also attended the historic session of the Congress at Amritsar in December 1919 and had an opportunity to meet many Congress leaders.

In 1916 when the author's first
article appeared in the Press

## 1916

|

## 1966

Some of the participants in the
Golden Jubilee celebrations of
the author as a Journalist
(April 8, 1966)

On account of such pre-occupations, I could not devote much attention to Law studies. Consequently, I could not get through the annual test. Those were also the days of the non-cooperation movement launched by Mahatma Gandhi. So, I succeeded in pursuing my brother not to press me to rejoin the Law College. Thus, I became free from the 'Varsity education at the age of twenty-six.

# CHAPTER 2

## Journalist in the Making

While I was getting increasingly disinclined to pursue my Law studies at Lahore, Lala Lajpat Roy, after his return from exile in America, started his famous daily newspaper, the *Bande Matram*. Like the Lion of Punjab, as Lalaji was popularly called, the *Bande Matram* soon Became a household word throughout the Urdu-knowing world. I felt deeply attracted by his powerful personality and equally powerful pen. Fortunately, I got an opportunity to come closer to him. I offered my services for a vacancy under him. A test was held and I was appointed as a sub-editor on the staff of the paper in early 1920. It was, indeed, my initiation in active journalism. But I could not stick there for long.

Awakening and bustle in Lahore, time and again, reminded me of the helplessness of the people of my own State. The question continuously itched me: if Lahore could provide scope for so many newspapers, could not the vast State of Jammu and Kashmir afford even a single newspaper? I often lost myself in building cloud castles of journalism in Jammu and Kashmir, while working in the Bande Matram. Once or twice getting leave from my office, I actually visited Jammu to study the local milieu and had the opportunity of talking to and discussing with my friends and elders about my ambition: What should be the name of the newspaper? What should be its readership? Wherefrom would come the material to sustain it? A friend was sceptical about the availability of so many news stories for the newspaper every week. Might not the paper, he inquisitively queried, have to be printed with some blank pages? Another sympathiser close to the Durbar circles warned that my attempt to bring out newspapers in the State might be regarded by powers that be, as an historic act against the State and I be dubbed as a rebel. All this, however, could not stand in the way of determination to have a newspaper in the State.

At last the time came when I bade good-bye to Lahore and settled down in Jammu. But I was penniless. My elder brother insisted that since I had spent one year in the Law college, I should obtain a license for legal practice, which one could get those days even without completing the law course. In deference to my brother's wishes I did submit an application to the High Court. It was rejected but it did satisfy my brother and me, too.

I was a jobless B.A. Securing permission for starting a newspaper seemed to be a Herculean task. Life in the town without a job is becoming impossible. I had also entered the marital life and did not want to be a financial burden on my brother any longer. In order, therefore, to meet my expenses I joined as an Accountant in the grade of Rs. 65-80 in the Private Estate, commonly known as Bhaderwah Jagir, of Maharaja (then Raja) Hari Singh. During the service, after office hours, I spent most of my time in the public library and also continued my efforts in making conditions favourable for a newspaper in the State. I was also shadowed by the police.

Finally came the moment when on Chet 9 Samvat 1977 corresponding to March 22, 1921, I submitted an application to His Highness Maharaja Pratap Singh for permission to start a newspaper and set up a printing press for that purpose. Under the Press law in vogue in the State in those days, only the Ruler, and no other authority, could grant such permission.

The application in Urdu ran: "With deep respect it is submitted that I belong to Samba town, Jammu District. I am a young-man of twenty-six and a graduate from Prince of Wales College. I have a natural liking for a journalistic career and have devoted much of my time in the study of journalism and its uses. It is my long-cherished desire to start a weekly from Jammu and to establish a printing press, too, to run the newspaper. It is requested that permission may kindly be granted under Rules 3 and 5 of the Press and Publications Regulations.

"It is mandatory under these Regulations to deposit a security deposit for the printing press and the newspaper. But it is very humbly sought that since it is for the first time that a newspaper will be started and a printing press set up in the State, Your Highness may in order to encourage the applicant in this noble task, exempt these from security.

"The aims and the object of the newspaper would be:

1. To promote feelings of loyalty and sympathy between the ruler and his people.
2. To publish the interesting, important and latest happenings in the State and the up-to-date main events of the world.

3. To promote feelings of unity and integrity amongst different sections and various classes of the people.
4. To channelise public opinion to beneficial purposes.
5. To place before the ruler the genuine grievances of the people for their proper redressal.
6. To discuss the educational, social, cultural, economic and other conditions of the State.

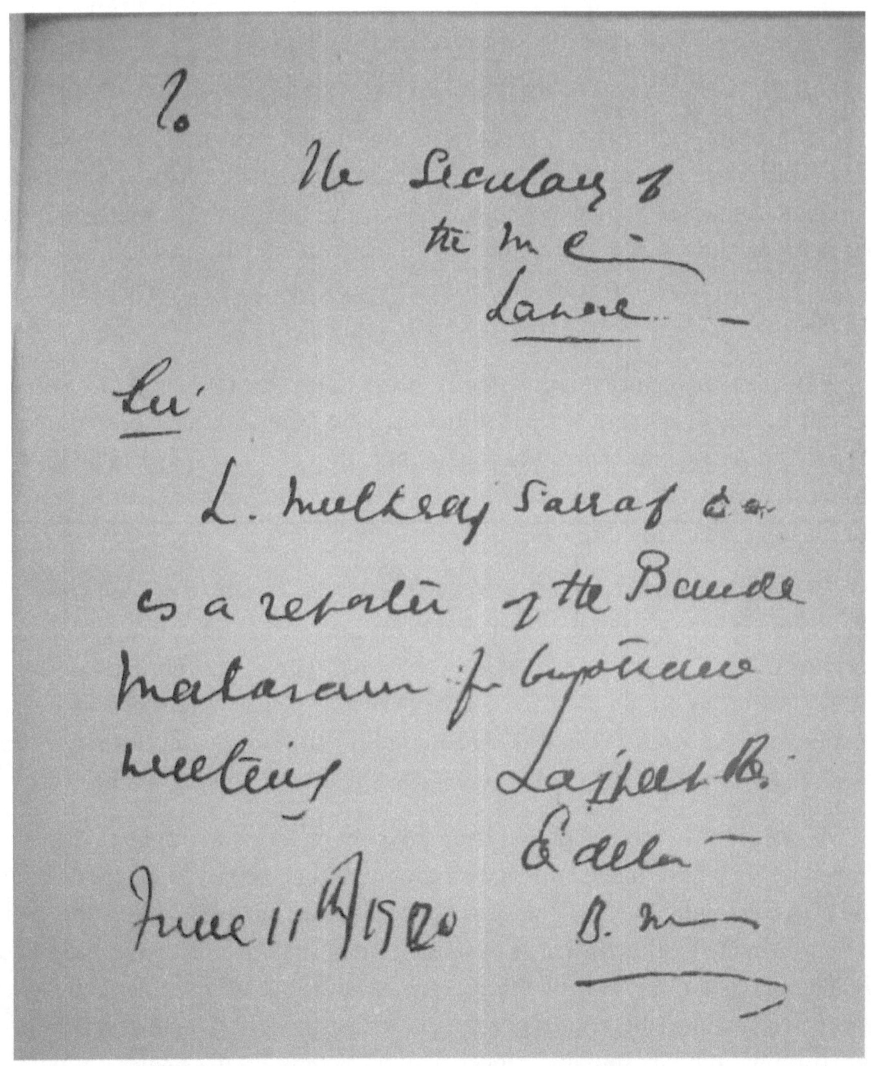

*A facsimile of Lala Lajpat Rai's handwriting*

Having made this application, I started propaganda bringing home to the leading public men the necessity of a newspaper in the State. I persistently wrote in the national press and exhorted some friends also to do the same, underlining how an educated Youngman of the State was determined to start a newspaper in the State for the first time.

Replying to my application, the Assistant Secretary to the Chief Minister, Jammu and Kashmir State, wrote to me under his office letter No 42 dated April 14, 1921: "With reference to his application dated Chet 9, Samvat 1977, Lala Mulk Raj Saraf is hereby informed that the Durbar does not consider it advisable to entertain his application for starting a weekly journal at Jammu".

On probing the matter I discovered that when my application was put before Maharaja Pratap Singh, he was personally highly delighted and in his own hand remarked on the application: "Since the time of my forefathers there has been no newspaper in the State. My Chief Minister Dewan Sahib, who is also my trusted advisor, should advise me as to what to do or what not do in the matter."

Rai Bahadur Major General Dewan Bishan Das was the Chief Minister of Jammu and Kashmir, and Rai Bahadur Lala Jagat Ram was his Secretary. Both of them opined against permitting the publication of a newspaper. Pandit Brij Mohan Dattatray Kaifi, the renowned Urdu poet, was the Assistant Secretary but his duty was limited to drafting Durbar fiats.

I was astounded to receive this Durbar order, but it did not discourage me. I kept up my spirits and publicly voiced protest against the order. I flayed it in the national press. This became the talk of the town. There was muffled talk even the royal Durbar which used to be held every day but where only privileged people had approach. This was considered an important development. On Baisakhi 29, Samvat 1978 (MAY 21, 1921), I proffered another application.

Asserting that "no reason has been given in rejecting my first application, therefore, I cannot make my submission on that score", I penned some additional grounds seeking the requisite permission, again in Urdu: "It is well known to your Highness that thousands of newspapers are being published all over India and several of them come under your study, too. They give information about the conditions in the country. Likewise newspapers are also running in many Indian (Princely) States which discuss matters of public importance. The concerned Princes and the authorities keep themselves informed through these newspapers and accordingly run administration and make various orders.

"This is also crystal clear that Your Highness desires to see your people progressing and prosperous by removing their genuine grievances and putting a stop to any excesses Achievements of this objective can be facilitated by a local newspaper. At present there is no channel for people's grievances to reach Your Highness. This shortcoming can be remedied by starting a newspaper from the State Capital so that genuine complaints continue receiving Your Highness's attention.

Whereas Your Highness evinces keen interest in foreign affairs, you have greater interest in your own people's conditions. Concocted news stories from the State are also carried in some irresponsible outside newspapers. A local newspaper would be an effective instrument in contradicting baseless propaganda. This will indeed be in the interest of both the ruler and the people of the State.

"The applicant is an educated State subject and fully understands his responsibilities. Applicant's purpose in starting a newspaper is to keep you informed about the conditions in the State as well as to benefit Your Highness's people by creating interest in education and improving their social and economic environment."

In reply, I received the following letter from the Assistant Secretary to Chief Minister under No. 3814 dated July 5, 1921: "His Highness the Maharaja Sahib Bahadur has ordered that the starting of a newspaper in the State cannot be allowed."

I did remonstrate the second refusal but found marked variance in this order from the first one which had stated that the Durbar did not consider it advisable to even advisable to entertain my application. The reply to the second application at least signified that my application had fortunately been both entertained and considered, though the decision was still against me. The alternation in the official tone was significant and considering it a step forward I continued my efforts unabated. On the auspicious day of Baisakhi 1, Samvat 1979, (April 13, 1922) I put in my application for the third time.

In this, I had repeated more or less the same submission as made in my first two petitions.Only one important sentence was added: "If in the period of current reforms such a newspaper was started from the State, this could be greatly instrumental for the betterment of the people of the State."

The word "reforms" was introduced in this application because the constitutional reforms were being inducted in the whole of British India and a period of reforms had also been initiated in the State. Maharaja Pratap Singh had been revested with full powers by the British Government. Dewan Bishan Das had retired as the Chief Minister and the reins of the Government had passed into the hands of Raja Sir Hari Singh as Senior and Foreign Minister.

It was generally believed that Raja Hari Singh favoured introduction of reforms in the State. However, my third application also met the same fate. Nevertheless the wording of Government refusal this time was comparatively less discouraging. This reply from the Secretary to Senior and Foreign Minister under No. 2010 dated 27-6-1922 read: "With reference to his application dated the 1st Baisakh 1979, regarding grant of permission to publish a weekly paper at Jammu, Lala Mulk Raj Saraf is hereby informed that His Highness the Maharaja Sahib Bahadur is not inclined to grant the required permission."

The reply to the first letter had stated that it was not even proper even to consider the application, the second application was considered but was not allowed and the reply to the third application reflected a grudging if not evasive attitude. Important changes, however, were taking place in the conditions in the State along with the varying national and international scenes which no Government could afford to ignore without endangering its own existence. The repeated refusal of the Government only seeded my will and that of my friends too. A sort of campaign was again launched in the national press protesting against the anti-press policy of the Durbar. The Dogra Sabha, then the solitary political organisation in the State, on being moved by me also stressed the need of starting a newspaper from the State.

I submitted my fourth application which proved to be the last on March 21, 1923 to the Senior and Foreign Minister, reiterating that publication of a newspaper from the State was indispensable and beneficial both for the Government and the people.

This application went to the Home Minister who pushed it on to the Commerce and Industries Minister, as the Planning Department was under him. Fortunately enough that portfolio was in the hands of an enlightened and liberal gentleman from Madras, Mr. Nagarkatti, while a popular bureaucrat Pandit Nand Lal Koul was his Secretary. But, Mr. Wakefield, a Britisher, was functioning as the Chief Secretary to Raja Hari Singh, the Senior and Foreign

Minister. This gentleman had great say in the Durbar: no matter could be put up in the Council of Ministers without first consulting him. When Mr. Nagarkatti brought my application to his notice that clever Briton privately queried from some people about my ideology and conduct. After completing necessary enquiries, Mr. Wakefield wrote in favour of putting up the matter in the Council.

However, before getting it into the Council agenda, Mr. Nagarkatti sent my application to the District Magistrate, Jammu, for his opinion about my character. This step was taken probably in view of my being *persona non grata* with the police who looked askance at me because of my activities to secure permission to start a newspaper in the State. Pandit Ram Chandra Dubey, the District Magistrate, in his wisdom forwarded my application to the Wazir Wazarat (Sub-divisional Magistrate) who sent it on to the *Tehsildar* who formally summoned me. On the due date I appeared in the Tehsil office and presented certificates about my education, qualification and character. Having examined them the *Tehsildar* wrote a note and forwarded it to the Wazir Wazarat who sent the dossier to the District Magistrate's office. The District Magistrate submitted the note with the remarks to the Minster. After scrutinising the papers, Mr. Nagarkatti drafted a resolution favouring permission and dispatched it to the Council.

As I came to know later when the resolution was put up in the Council. Mr. B.J. Glancy I.C.S. Minister In-charge Police and Finance Departments (who later became the Governor of the pre-1947 undivided Punjab) had first opposed it and then advised that if the editor of the paper undertook the responsibility to regularly contradict all such news and dispatches as appeared to outside Press against the State and the British authorities and also to continue to support the State Government, he might be granted the permission sought for. In other words the permission for the newspaper was to be only for publishing articles favouring the State Government. Mr. Nagarkatti, however, pointed out the progress that the world had made and remarked that the important events were taking place in the international area, in view of which permission for starting a newspaper within the State was bound to benefit the Government and its people. Yet while expressing his opinion in favour of granting the permission he, inter alia, noted on my application that it should be made clear to applicant that "he would write in his paper only on such matters as would lead to educational, economic and industrial advancement and that he would not use his pen to create class hatred and communal dissensions or arouse religious susceptibilities and that it was also expected of the applicant that he would not refrain from writing on such matters of political nature as would adversely affect relations of Jammu and Kashmir with the British Government or any other Indian State."

Luckily it was the heart-felt desire of Maharaja Pratap Singh to see a newspaper published in the State like those published in the Punjab. Raja Hari Singh, the Senior And Foreign Minister was also not opposed to it and Mr. Nagarkatti had already given his mind and supported it. Therefore, when this matter was finally discussed in the State Council on March 18, 1924, the Council unanimously accepted my application to which the Maharaja also subsequently affixed the Royal Seal.

Acting wisely, the State Council while granting permission to start a paper did not consider it proper to restrict me in any manner as was suggested by Messer Glancy and Nagarkatti. The order that I got was in fact in the form of a letter that Mr. Nagarkatti had communicated to the Governor (District Magistrate) Jammu and a copy of which he had sent to me under his own signatures. This letter No. 12488 dated March 28, 1924, read: With reference to your letter No. A1748 dated 31st January, 1924, I have the honour to inform you that His Highness the Maharaja Sahib Bahadur in the Council has been pleased to accord permission under section 5 of the Jammu and Kashmir Press and Publications Regulations of 1971 Bikrami to request that you will kindly take the necessary action in the matter according to the provisions of the Jammu and Kashmir Press and Publications Regulation of 1971."

Along with seeking permission for the newspaper I had also applied for the permission for setting up a printing press. The above letter, however, did not mention anything about the printing press. I. therefore addressed a letter to the Commerce and Industries Minister on April 1, 1924, requesting that I should be assured that the permission for starting the newspaper included the permission for starting a printing press as well. The very next day, that is on April 2, 1924, I received the order No. 12652 stating: "With reference to your application of yesterday's date, I have the honour to inform you that the permission already conveyed to you implies permission for starting a press also." Thereafter, the State Council at its meeting in Srinagar on June 5, 1924, confirmed this reply of the Commerce and Industries Minister.

The Governor (District Magistrate) of Jammu in the light of the State Council Resolution of March 18, 1924, sent a memo to me on April 25,

1924 directing: "Lala Mulk Raj Saraf may be asked to fulfil the condition as laid down in section 3 and 13 of the Press and Publications Regulation. He may furnish a cash security of Rs. 500.00". In compliance with this order I deposited Rs, 500.00 as the security on the following day viz. April 25, 1924. I had already submitted the declaration for the press and newspaper as soon as I had received the Government's order. The Government replied to me on May 5, 1924 under No. 726: "With reference to his letter No. Nil dated The 26th April, 1924, to the address of the District Magistrate, Lala Mulk Raj Saraf is hereby have duly been accepted under the F.D. Receipt No. 856/769 dated the 26th April, 1924, After the Council permission Rs. 500.00 deposited by him in the Punjab National Bank as pledged security has been kept with the Nazir of this office for safe custody."

Thus, after all, having passed through various stages over a period of more than three years, I was fortunate enough to get the permission to start the first newspaper from the Jammu and Kashmir State.

After the Council permission, one day Mr, Nagarkatti called me to his office and made some queries from me about the policy of the newspaper. Having got appropriate replies he expressed his satisfaction. I vividly recollect his words: "This permission is a test whether a State subject could discharge such a public responsibility especially in these trying times." I remembered the God Almighty and prayed to Him to enable me to come out successfully in the test.

# CHAPTER 3

# The Ranbir Takes Shape

In the beginning I had intended to name the paper "Pahari" and the press "Dogra Press". But after further consideration I thought it proper to name the newspaper "Ranbir" and the press "Public Printing Press". No doubt, the newspaper title with the name of late Maharaja Ranbir Singh, son of Maharaja Gulab Singh who was the founder of the Jammu and Kashmir State, and the father of kind hearted and generous Maharaja Pratap Singh. He was considered a wide awake and learned ruler. But in reality "Ranbir" was "Ranvir" literally meaning 'Knight of the Battlefield'.

The feeling, however, soon began to dawn upon me that getting permission for starting a newspaper was perhaps not so hard a job as actually publishing the paper and putting it on a sound footing. Numerous friends conveyed their felicitations to me as they felt overjoyed at my success in obtaining the permission for a newspaper. It was as if they had come upon something long due to them. They pressed hard that the Ranbir should be started as soon as possible: just as I had been pressing the Government for granting the permission. But I had to literally start from a scratch.

With a view to carrying out the new task I naturally gave up the Government service. Arranging funds seemed an intractable proposition. My ambitions were high but resources were very little. I had spent quite a few years in struggling hard to obtain the permission for starting the newspaper. The people also appeared restive to see the first newspaper of their State but good intentions alone would not, as indeed these could not, provide me the wherewithal to proceed further with the venture.

Some newspapers in Punjab began to take serious exception to the delay in publishing the newspaper after getting the much sought after permission. At first, I thought of floating a limited company but its success looked doubtful, as the moneyed persons were only interested in their lucre. On the other hand my sole motive in starting the newspaper was to serve the State according to my own ideas.

After a good deal of thought, I found a like-minded friend Mr. Vishwa Nath Wadehra, who accepted my offer of managing the newspaper. When the question of expenses came, I immediately put before him all the ornaments of my wife. He was deeply moved. Instead of utilizing the jewellery, Mr. Wadehra, immediately ran to common friend Wazir Tej Ram and borrowed Rupees Two Thousand from him. The pronote was jointly signed by both of us. Thus I got a valuable colleague as well as the necessary finance.

Then began a search for the office and the printing press. We got a small cutcha quarter near the Rani Talab belonging to Thakur Kartar Singh who later rose to be the State's Finance Minister. We set up a hand litho printing press for which we obtained the services of a machine-man from Sialkot. A few more technicians had to be recruited. Those available were mostly the permanent employees of the local Government Press, then called the Ranbir Prakash Press but now named as the Ranbir Government Press. They were ultimately prevailed upon to work after the office hours. There were also no *Katibs* (calligraphists) at that time. Again we had to depend upon the official machinery. Munshi Taj Din was a renowned *Katib* employed in the Government Press. He and one of his juniors undertook to do the job for Ranbir. Taj Din would not, however, come to our office. We had to take the necessary material to him at his house. We gladly withstood thus humouring him. With great difficulty we later on secured services of two whole-time *Katibs*.

The appointment of the editorial and managerial staff offered no handicaps. Mr. Wadehra was the manager and I the editor. There was no question of appointing any assistant in the very beginning. In clerical jobs, both of us were trained and we did the work of even folding the paper ourselves as an austerity measure.

Notwithstanding all this, we did need a person for going out, cleansing offices, distributing the paper, etc. Luckily, we got the services of a thorough honest, loyal, and untiring man in the person of Pandit Jagat Ram. His loyalty was so abiding that when after having served in the Ranbir office for twenty-six years, the newspaper was wound up, he did not leave me till he breathed his last at over eighty. He continued to serve me with the same dedication that had been his hallmark throughout. He worked as a peon in the office, he made purchases from the market, he distributed newspapers to the local subscribers and also collected the subscription. Whenever he got some leisure, he did not shirk any domestic job and even supervised the children. He was intolerant of any shoddy work or any loss. All the big and the small in the office and the household held him in great reverence like an esteemed elder of the family.

Having established the office but before setting up our printing press, a life-size Urdu poster was issued in the name of the Manager, Mr. Wadehra, since there was no private press in Jammu, this poster was printed on payment from Government Press. The poster carried a long caption:- "True interpreters of the national sentiments, the Weekly Ranbir, will soon come out from the Rajdhani Jammu in solemn dignity." It said "Respectable citizens, thousand thanks to the God Almighty that our long-cherished hope has been realised. His Highness the Maharaja Bahadur and the Members of the State Council, much kindness have fulfilled a long-desired object of the people of the State and keeping in view their future welfare, permitted the publication of a national Weekly from the State. The first editor, printer and publisher of the Ranbir will be a qualified young man, Mr. Mulk Raj Saraf, B.A. What the paper would be like, will be evident from the paper itself. However, for the information of the people, it would be proper to say that the policy of the Ranbir will be similar to that of a national paper. It will not hold brief for any particular religion or sect but it will be the common mouthpiece of the people of the State irrespective of religion, caste or creed.

"The Ranbir will provide fresh and trustworthy news from all parts of the State, will place the requirements of the people before the country and the ruler and inter alia discuss the social, cultural, educational, commercial, agricultural and other economic affairs pertaining to the State. Weighty writings of well-known scribes and correspondents from inside and outside the State will adorn its pages and compositions of competent poets appearing in it will entertain the reader. Arrangements will be made to have latest and useful news from all foreign countries in general and from India and Indian States in particular. In short no pains would be spared to make the newspaper inviting.

"We are fully confident that the first national newspaper of the State will reach every literate person in the State and the public will encourage the management by paying advance subscription or accepting to have the first newspaper sent to them by V.P.P. The newspaper will also have its own printing press. The subscription rate of the newspaper will be rupees four per annum and rupees two and annas eight for six months. Every issue will be priced at an anna and a half,

"The Ranbir will be *sui generis* in the advancement of business of the advertisers. The advertisement rates will be an anna and a half per line for the first line and an anna per line subsequently. Those wishing to advertise should immediately dispatch their material. Other details could be settled orally or through correspondence. All business correspondence should be with the manager and all contributions for publication should be sent to the editor."

As soon as the poster was published, the public began to manifest practical proof of their deep interest in the project. The itch among the people to read their own first newspaper was so intense that they vied with one another by sending in the subscription.

Some of the prominent people who honoured us by remitting their subscriptions before the actual appearance of the paper included Pandit Jia Lal Koul Kilam Vakil, Sardar Khem Chand, Officer-in-Charge Tosha Khanna and his son Dr. Barkat Ram, Mirza Ghulam Mustafa, Aga Syed Hussain. Pandit Shri Kanth Thusso, Lala Sukhram Dass Shah, Lala Durga Dass Gandotra, Pandit Ganga Ram Sub Judge, Pandit Govind Ram Sub-Divisional Magistrate, Lala Bal Chand Gupta, Shri Salig Ram Koul Vakil, Pandit Srinivas Shah, Thakur Haqiqat Singh Jamwal, Moulavi Mohd. Abdullah Vakil, Pandit Chander Joo Vakil, Pandit Govind Joo, Sardar Kanhaiya Singh, Lala Bodh Raj, Pandit Lok Nath Sharma Vakil, Lala Dina Nath Gandotra, Home Secretary, Pandit Lakhmi Chand Magotra, Shri Ram Nath Kapoor, Manager Dewans' Estate, Thakur Sardool Singh, Director, Rafi-ud-Din, Lala Kashmiri Lal Gaind, Lala Badri Nath Mirpuri, Wazir Asu Ram, Pandit Banke Bihari, Pandit Bholoo Ram, Lala Beli Ram, Jyotshi Anant Ram, Ram Vakil, Mahasha Ram Chand Gupta and Thakur Lala Boota Mal Transporter, Sardar Sunder Singh Rais, Shri Ganesh Das Headmaster, Chaudhri Mangtu Shah, Shri Mehboob Alam Inspector Police, Lala Shiv Nath Vakil, Lala Nathu Ram Vakil, Mahasha Ram Chand Gupta and Thakur Dhanantar Singh Salathia, Forest Range Officer who sent ten rupees instead of four as yearly subscription and continued doing that for many years.

Maharaja Pratap Singh donated one hundred annually while Sir Raja Hari Singh rupees fifty annually for "this pioneer enterprise' as remarked in the official letter to me.

This sampling of the original subscribers of the Ranbir would show how the people of the State, particularly the young men, in all walks of life and in all parts of the State, were enthused with the emergence of the first newspaper in their minds. Many of them later played a significant part in making the State tread onward and indeed rose to eminent positions in their respective spheres. This reflected the presence, though in a latent form, of sufficient social urge and awakening among the people who needed some forum to project their views and the Ranbir did indeed amply prove it. Their continued association with the Ranbir was, no doubt, a source of mutual inspiration and guidance.

In addition to the towns, numerous messages were pouring from the far-off places enquiring impatiently when the Ranbir will be out. We, on our part, were planning durable arrangements so that once started, the newspaper shall continue to function.

Those days it was not so difficult to obtain the postal registration number as it is now. Such registration reduces the postage expenses. I arranged the registration number at Lahore for the very first issue of the Ranbir. It is an interesting story as to how this happened. We were anxious to cut down the expenses to the minimum. I hit upon the proposal to issue a dummy issue of the Ranbir. This sample edition was published on May 20, 1924, corresponding to *Jaishth 8, Samvat* 1981. It front-paged a poem captioned "Oh restive heart of the nation, hold on steadfastly." It was a beautiful composition by a kind friend and renowned poet of the Punjab, Pandit Har Krishan Lal Habib Wazirabadi. The front page also contained an article by Shri Chuni Lal Anand forcefully pointing out that the Shri Mahalakshmi Temple, Pacca Danga, in the heart of the Jammu City, was the headquarter of '*Churrus wallas*' who worshipped the *churrus* day and night.

The leading article in the sample issue was titled "Righteousness". Besides other things the article highlighted the significance of the word "Ranbir". Its lexical meaning was "Knight of the battlefield"; 'Rana' meant the battlefield and 'Vir' signified puissant vanquisher by nature. The word 'Napoleon', in French means the same thing as the word "Ranbir" in Sanskrit.

There was another poem inside captioned, "The Ranbir is not a mere scrap of paper" a composition by Syed Zulfiqar Ali Nasim Razvi asserting that the "Ranbir" would heartily support the common cause of the Hindus and the Muslims and whatever it would say, would not be word-fencing or prolix. The dummy edition carried another important item. It was the Urdu rendering of the four-year-old historical address by the Governor General of

India., Lord Chelmsford, which he had delivered in Jammu in 1921, on the occasion of the restoration of full powers to Maharaja Pratap Singh.

I took the edition to Lahore and approached the office of the Postmaster General where after due scrutiny I was at once given the registered number L-1677 for the Ranbir.

Now came the important stage of having reporters and correspondents for Ranbir. It required deep consideration as to how to arrange for collection and dispatch of the news from the important places of the State. Those days there were very few people in the State who had any experience in reporting. A reporter is concerned with facts and nothing but facts. He may like or dislike a fact, he may agree or disagree with any step by a public leader or a Government spokesman but as a press correspondent, he is duty-bound to project the factual picture without exaggeration and distortion leaving it to hide readers to draw their own conclusions. The five-word Bible of journalists namely "facts are sacred, comments free" was then little known in the State.

Fortunately, however, we had not to face much difficulty in this respect in view of our own limited requirements. From the very start we could get the services of some sincere young men with little experience but deep sense of public service. And the wonder of wonders was that they did not expect nor were paid any remuneration. Believe it or not those correspondents of the Ranbir used to pay for reading their own stories as they regularly paid the subscription of the paper.

The foremost correspondent of the Ranbir was Maulvi Mohd. Zain-ul-Abdin Kohi Samahanvi. He used to send news and other stories concerning Mirpur district including Bhimber and Kotli (now under Pakistan occupation) as well as Nowshera and Rajouri. He used to write under different pen-names, sometimes his full name, sometimes only 'Samhanvi', at other times 'Majzub Kisan' and occasionally under 'Mirpur District Correspondent'. in his first letter to the editor published in the Ranbir, he asked the Ruler "If Your Highness is keenly interested to know about the miserable conclusions under which the people of the State live, then please do not enquire from the zaildars who like quakes are themselves are mostly responsible for the ills of the rural population. These zaildars are at best the spokesmen of the Government but they cannot rightly represent the down-trodden people. If

Your Highness wants to be acquainted with the true state of affairs concerning the hut-dweller and the half-naked farmer, then kindly ask such a man in person in person as to how he finds the world or read what appears in the columns of the Ranbir."

With the passage of time, the Ranbir was able to secure the services of some competent and reliable correspondents. Here are some prominent names among them:

**Srinagar:** Pandit Salig Ram Koul Vakil, Pandit Jia Lal Koul Kilam Advocate, Maulvi Mohd. Abdullah Vakil, Pandit Prem Nath Bazaz, Pandit Kashyap Bandhu, Pandit Prem Nath Sadhu Pardesi, Pandit Baldev Prashad Sharma, Shri Thakur Singh Das and Mr. K.N. Aima.

| | | |
|---|---|---|
| **Sopore** | : | Munshi Ghulam Rasul Khadim |
| **Baramulla** | : | Sardar Kanhaiya Singh |
| **Muzaffarabad** | : | Lala Ram Lal Shah and Lala Bodh Raj |
| **Bhaderwah** | : | Kotwal Ram Lal |
| **Kishtwar** | : | Mehta Nand Lal, Shri Ishrat Kashmiri and Shri Nishat Kishtwari |
| **Udhampur** | : | Lala Prahlad Bhagat Vakil |
| **Mirpur** | : | Chaudhri Gian Chand Sadabarti |
| **Ranbir Singh Pura** | : | Lala Roshlu Ram |
| **Bhimber** | : | Shri Chaman Lal Wadehra and Choudhry Mohd. Shafi |
| **Manawar** | : | Raizada Hans Raj Bali |
| **Samba** | : | Mahasha Ram Chand Gupta |
| **Kathua** | : | Lala Nathu Ram Vakil |
| **Kotli** | : | Bhagat Roop Chand Vakil and Munshi Chanan Din |
| **Rajouri** | : | Master Abdul Aziz Ilayi, Mirza Faquir Mohd and Chaudhri Mohan Lal Motial |

| | | |
|---|---|---|
| **Ramnagar** | : | Master Hem Raj Jandial |
| **Poonch** | : | Khawaja Ghulam Qadir Bandey and Shri Dayanand Kapoor |
| **Chenani** | : | Lala Dina Nath Gupta |

The renowned poet of Kashmir, Mahjoor, also occasionally used to send news to Ranbir. Shri Jawan Lal, a Police Court Inspector author of 'Hoe to prevent traffic in Women' used to write occasionally for the Ranbir. Similarly Pandit Ganga Nath Sharma who was on the personal staff of Maharaja Pratap Singh used to send important Durbar news and other stories.

So far as Jammu city, the seat of the Ranbir, was concerned, a number of correspondents, poets and other contributors, freely wrote for the Ranbir. They included Sarvashri Vishwanath Kerni, Zulfikar Ali Nasim, Habibullah, Shri Ram, Badri Nath Vakil, Girdhari Lal Anand, S.S. Nishat, Sarwan Nath Aftab, Prem Nath Sadhu Raunaq, Arjan Singh Arsh, Bansi Lal Suri, Kisha Samailpuri, Qais Sherwani, Manohar Lal Suri, Manohar Lal Dil, Mathra Das Shaiq, Mirza Mubarak Beg, Ram Kishen Ghafil, Master Zinda Koul, Narsingh Sahai Chauhan, Sahibzada Mohd. Umar, Mohiuddin Ahmad Qumar and Gosain Tara Chand. Besides, Lala Hans Raj Vakil, Sardar Budh Singh, Pandit Anant Ram Dogra, Pandit Lok Nath Sharma, Sardar Mohinder Singh, Lala Ram Saran Das Malhotra, Pandit Pindi Das Goswami, Thakur Kahan Singh Billowaria, Dr. Hari Chand Hari, Pandit Nand Lal Talib, Sardar Daleep Singh landlord and Raizada Lakhmi Chand contributed occasionally to the columns of the Ranbir. An eminent Urdu poet and writer, Pandit Vitasta Prasad Fida of Lahore was one of the regular contributors from outside the State. Kaviraj Guru Dutt Vaid Sharma used to write from Karachi.

# CHAPTER 4

## A Red-Letter Day

June 24, 1924, corresponding to Har 11, Samvat 1981, will indeed be remembered as a red-letter day in the history of Jammu and Kashmir. It was then that the first regular issue of the Ranbir made its appearance. It was to be published every week in Urdu, the official language of the State. By happy coincidence, on that auspicious day, my wife who had gone to see her parents in Lyallpur (now in West Pakistan) gave birth to my second son, Suraj.

Besides, of course, the editorial and other items usually associated with a weekly newspaper, the inaugural twelve-page issue carried articles and compositions by Lala Hans Raj Vakil, Sardar Budh Singh, Pandit Har Kishan Lal Habib, Syed Zu-ul-Fikar Ali Nasim Razvi, Moulavi Mohd. Zain-ul-Abdin Kohli Samahnavi, Pandit Ram Saran Das Shandalia, Editor the Rajasthan and Dr. Barkat Ram (then in London). Another feature was 'A Lazy Nationalist'. His real name was not published. He was a great intellectual and a patriot. It may not be out of place to reproduce here some of his sentiments:

"To-day is undoubtedly a red-letter day in the history of Jammu and Kashmir. This is the 'Id' day which dawns after penance in the shape of fasting during the month of Ramzan, for the eleven months of mundane sins and other distracting activities. It signifies focus on the politics, culture and welfare of the State and lighting up the narrow crannies of moral and social degradations. All felicitations to the young man Lala Mulk Raj Saraf who has succeeded today in setting his foot after years of strenuous efforts and relentless struggle on the path which though full of pathos will take him to the goal of his ideals. Congratulations also to the Dogra community who is putting this heavy burden of its own welfare in various respects on the shoulders of this upcoming young man. It is a day of congratulations also for His Highness in whose reign this sapling is being planted which has the potential of growing into a strong shady tree capable of bearing fruits. But in order to nourish this plant, all shall have to devote their best energies and water it with their sweat and blood. That end has got to be achieved not by securing franchise on communal basis nor for loot and plunder, nor for usurping one another's human, social or political rights but for guaranteeing comforts to all the inhabitants their progress and prosperity and for the full development of all their mental and physical capacities."

Lala Hans Raj Vakil who was the founder of the first national organisation of the State viz. Dogra Sabha, as well as several other public institutions, felt ecstatic at the very idea of the publication of the first newspaper of the State. He wrote: "O, the desires of the main disheartened so far, are going to be realised: I am joyed beyond all limits to know that Ranbir is about to come out."

The first issue also contained three pages of advertisements. It would be of interest to recall the names of some of the advertisers of those days such as Bagai Motor Works, Jammu, Harrison and Co. Calcutta, Mangal Singh and Bros., Harmonium Makers, Jammu; Har Bhagwan Pansari, Rawalpindi, The Kashmir Kishore Pharmacy, Jammu; Karkhana Khizabe-Alam-Gir, Lyallpur; Secretary, Indian Mutual Family Relief Fund S.C.S. Amritsar and Lala Parmeshri Das Khosla M.A. Chief Agent, Jammu and Kashmir, the Lakshmi Insurance Co. Ltd., Lahore.

The idea to earn any profit from subscriptions and advertisements was far from my heart at that time. The receipts were meant only to meet the normal expenses. As the income of the newspaper began to increase, its staff also increased. The Ranbir had on its staff Hindus and Muslims, both Degras and Kashmiris as also people from the Punjab.

The quoin of the first issue of the Ranbir was of course its editorial underscoring the aims and objectives of the paper. Some excerpts of the editorial captioned 'Our Policy and Objectives' translated from Urdu are worth mentioning here:

"A new era is dawning upon the world and every nation and country is striving for progress. In some countries kingship holds away while at other places freedom struggle is being relentlessly pursued. In certain countries imperialism is reigning supreme while heads are bowing before democracy. If in some places commerce is thriving, in the other places capitalists and labourers are at loggerheads. Some places are even now steeped in darkness while others are seeing the struggle for social emancipation. If unity is the watchword somewhere, the idea of separate franchise is confronting in other areas. In some spots religious fanaticism was raising its head and in other parts proselytism was trumpeting. In short, every place is in ferment. Everywhere political, economic and social forces are pushing ahead and pulsating with new life. It is impossible that Jammu and Kashmir, somnolent for a long time, should remain unaffected by every day international happenings and the people in the State are so infused with the vigorous idea of marching forward. It is the symbol of awakening.

*The Title Page of the very first issue of the RANBIR*
*dated June 24, 1924*

"However, mere wishes could not lead to progress or bring one successfully out of struggle. Success demands sacrifice, perseverance, love, intrepidity and a course of action based on righteousness.

"That is the pious objective that brings Ranbir into the battlefield. Though it seems that the Ranbir is surrounded on all sides by thorny hedges, yet its own path is quite clear and straight: its motive force is duty, truth and dare. It is actuated by sentiments of service and love and it is far away from bias, hatred and underhand means; hence, fully convinced of its success.

"We will prefer the ancient system of Government through Panchayats to any other. The real inhabitants of the State should get their natural rights and they should have precedence in all spheres. But along with them the rights of those who have settled here for long or who have given up their homelands for settlement here or who during their settlement here had done their best in the service to the people of the State, should also be specially cared for.

"No country can forge ahead without complete unity and solidarity among its people. Advantages of unity are myriad. It is, therefore, imperative that the rights of every citizen, without caring for whether he is a Hindu or a Muslim or whether he is a Kashmiri or Dogra, should be fully and equally respected and guarded. This will eliminate any chance of mutual suspicion. However, we do not support any viewpoint which reflects separatism, and which is despised by the civilized world. In our view all people, whether Hindus or Muslims or whether they are Dogras, Kashmiris, Baltis or Ladakhis, are of equal status and whosoever among them is capable or acquitted himself well in any position has alone the right to occupy that position.

"We stand for free primary education throughout the State. Religious education may also be provided. Arrangements should be made for adequate industrial training to exploit the vast natural resources of the State.

"The Ranbir will particularly highlight the problem of social welfare. In this behalf people shall have to root out wisely and resolutely all those evils that are increasingly undermining the society and bringing us discredit and infamy in the world. Besides, we shall vigorously remedy the causes responsible for the social and moral deterioration of the people, in particular of those living in hilly areas.

"Following matters will be specially advocated by the Ranbir:

1.  Abolition of system of beggar (forced labour) which is reminiscent of the barbaric ages
2.  Eradication of corruption which is ravaging numerous poor and noble families
3.  Obliteration of perpetration of terrorism on the people of the State, particularly in the hills
4.  Removal of the rural indebtedness
5.  Financial, commercial, agricultural and industrial progress of the people
6.  Development of means of communication
7.  Adoption of adequate measures for the health of the people.

The concluding lines of this leading article said:

"In the progress of the people of the State lies the secret of the progress of the rest of India because this State is the head and the rest of India, the body. Therefore, whereas the Ranbir will be the well-wisher of the people of the State, it will also be equally helpful and friendly to the rest of India and would spare nothing in serving her. O God, do bless us and give us the power to succeed in these tests to perform your Commands."

The people received the first issue of the Ranbir with robust enthusiasm. The educated people gave it a place in their hearts. The villagers enjoyed reading it in groups. I received congratulatory messages even from London, Paris, New York, Hong Kong, Kabul and Baghdad where several youths of the State as also other friends happened to be at that moment.

Renowned storywriter Munshi Prem Chand expressed his great pleasure on the birth of the Ranbir 'from a far-off place like Jammu.' The well-known revolutionary Lala Har Dayal sent his message from Sweden describing the birth of the Ranbir as a significant event in the history of the Indian States. Newspapers in various parts of India approvingly reviewed the Ranbir in their columns. Munshi Mohammad Din Fauq, Editor, the Kashmir Magazine, Lahore, wrote: "From a country lacking a sense of appreciation for literature, to dive out such a valuable pearl was within the competence of *Saraf* (jeweller) alone."

Prominent among the poets who verified their ideas on the inauguration of the Ranbir included Shri Krishan Smailpuri, Lala Badrinath Vakil who later became the Law Secretary to the State Government, Syed Zulfiqar Ali Nasim who later became a *tehsildar* and is now holding a prominent position in West Pakistan, Pandit Prem Nath Pardesi, Pandit Har Kishan Lal Habib, Mirza Mubarak Beg Mubarik and Shri Ram Krishan Ghafil.

Among the numerous messages of greetings, there was one which I still cherish the most. It was from one of my esteemed teachers Shri Rattan Lal Mohan. He was the first graduate teacher at whose feet I had had the privilege to sit and learn much during my school days. He was passionately devoted to literature and journalism which later impelled him to resign from the education department and settle in Lahore. There, Shri Mohan came in contact with several prominent newspapers and other periodicals. His highly literary and informative articles appeared in various leading newspapers under the pen name of 'An unknown journalist'. During the First World War, he also served as an interpreter in the Middle East.

When Shri Mohan learnt that an old pupil of his had laid the foundations of Journalism in Jammu and Kashmir, he sent me a lengthy letter giving valuable tips which, even though over forty years have since gone by, can still prove guideposts for the journalists today. The letter which is dated Lahore, July 1, 1924, exactly a week after the appearance of the Ranbir, said: "I hasten to congratulate you on the bringing out of the Ranbir. The sturdy infant shall one day rise to the full proportions of a highly developed institution and you cannot be too careful to bestow your undivided attention to its growth. Let your tone be serious rather than idealistic, practical rather than commonplace and sympathetic rather than hyper-critical. But guard yourself against being too grave, pontifical and patriarchal. Infuse humour into your notes, make them light but not flippant. Be always on the side of law, order and constitutionalism. Let your style be vigorous, not flamboyant; simple, not jejune; direct, not blunt; let it strike a happy medium between the plain and the ornate. Do not use such words as *Sansani Khej* which is nonsense. Study regularly some high-class Urdu journals such as the zamindar or some other magazines. Make a discriminating use of new terms of speech. Do not let the passion get the better of your reason. You cannot cleanse the world of its evil by a stroke of the pen, however vigorous it may be. Remember to climb down from the cloud-land of the ideals to hard facts. Never permit your criticism to be bitter or one-sided. Needless to add that you know the intention of the

Defamation Act. Do not publish unauthorised communications. But I need not play the part of a preacher to you. Your qualifications, public spirit and the stern integrity of your motives shall make you equal to the exigencies of journalistic life. I wish you the best of luck, Cheerio."

# CHAPTER 5

## Encounters With the Wrong Doers

True to its profession, the Ranbir had, since its very inception, to wage its relentless struggle against all those elements who stood in the way of a healthy development of community life. Indeed, no public service is possible with a sense of fear and favour. A conscientious worker in any walk of life, at times, is bound to suffer the wrath of the authority; at other times, the anger of the ignorant public; and still on occasions the obstinacy of the both together. Naturally, the Ranbir could not be an exception. It always had its share of bouquets as well as brickbats. What, however, appeared to me to be more than compensating was the sort of spiritual bliss that I invariably felt over each encounter with the wrong doers. Some such interesting experiences in the early life of Ranbir may be mentioned here.

It was the time of Maharaja Pratap Singh. The cooks of the Royal Household used to bring their *hookahs* with them during working hours. After finishing the job, dishonest cooks would empty the basin of their *hookahs* and refill them with Ghee and then leave the precincts of the royal kitchen. The Ranbir criticised the conduct of such cooks, of course, in light vein. When in obedience to royal command, I presented myself in the Durbar, His Highness generously asked me to take my seat near him and then in low yet sublime voice told me that he was never unaware of what was happening in his kitchen but since I had given it publicity and voiced public feelings in the matter, he ordered his personal secretary to honour me with an award of Rs. 200.00 (equivalent to the cost of a robe of honour) as token of his appreciation. At first, I hesitated to accept the money but on being affectionately reprimanded by some kind friends present there, that my refusal to accept the royal pleasure would tantamount to an act of discourtesy to the person of august Ruler, I agreed, put the cash into my pocket, bowed before His Highness and returned home.

Mr. B.J. Glancy, the Finance and Police Minister, generally used to go to Lahore on weekends. Once a deputation headed by Sheikh Sadiq Hussain, a leading member of the Central Legislative Assembly, waited upon him in Lahore and placed before him grievances and demands of Muslims of Jammu and Kashmir. A comprehensive account of this meeting appeared in the civil and military Gazette Lahore of June 6, 1925. The reply given by Mr. Glancy to deputations as published in the Lahore Daily indicated that the whole affair concerning the deputation was probably stage-managed at the instance of Mr. Glancy himself. While answering the questions put by the Lahore deputation on behalf of the Muslims population of the State, Mr. Glancy posed himself not merely as the champion of their cause but also the virtual Ruler of the State. Some of his replies besides being seemingly inspired were most overweening. I could hardly believe that an experienced administrator that undoubtedly Mr. Glancy could allow himself to conduct like that. I waited for over a week to see if any contradiction of the reported statement would be forthcoming but it was in vain. I, then, took up the cudgels, challenged the statement of Mr. Glancy, which besides being derogatory to the Maharaja, was capable of inciting communal passions. I vehemently attacked him for expressing partisan views to the detriment of the interests of the people of the State as a whole. The day (Har 32, 1982) my comments appeared in the Ranbir, Major (now Lieutenant Colonel) Baldev Singh Samyal, who was A.D.C. to Raja Hari Singh, Senior and Political Member of the State Council and also holding the rank of the Commander-in-Chief of the State Forces, came to me to convey Raja Sahib's appreciation of my article criticising Mr. Glancy. Soon after, the same day, Major-General Thakur Janak Singh, Revenue Minister, paid a visit to my office and patted on my back. All sections of the public opinion spoke highly of these comments, Muslims not excluding.

As a matter of fact, the Ranbir from the very start held the view that there was no such thing as Muslim grievances or Hindu grievances. Nobody would deny the existence of then as even now but such grievances are more or less common to all and hence are people's grievances which could be remedied by common efforts of the responsible people. Such attitude of the Ranbir, however, also aroused jealousy of some 'friends' and they approached Mr. Glancy who infuriated over the comments in the Ranbir. He rushed to the State Council with a strongly worded note stressing urgency to launch proceedings on behalf of the State against the Editor of the Ranbir "for the affront indulged by him in his paper against a Minister of the State Government." The pity of it was that the State Council gave its consent to carry out the behest of its all-powerful British Minister. What actually took place inside the Council Chamber, I never bothered to enquire about. It was anybody's guess. The Council order, however, then to be effective, required the Ruler's assent. When the case was put up before Maharaja Pratap Singh, he mutely, as was his wont, asked the State Secretary to read out to him the Editor's reply to the charges against him. The Secretary searched through the file more than once but could find no trace there of any query from the Editor much less a reply thereto. Thereupon His Highness observed that it did not behove the royalty to sign an order of prosecution against a person without first giving him an opportunity to reply. He was not at all, he added, in favour of condemning the unheard. So, the file was sent back to the Council with the instructions from His Highness to first attach an explanation of the Editor with the papers and then seek his assent.

The Council Secretariat forwarded the file to the District Magistrate, Jammu. I was summoned by the District Magistrate (Pandit Ram Chandra Dubey). When I appeared before his court, he gently enquired of me as to why I dared offend Mr. Glancy. I simply replied that it was my bounden duty to criticise his public conduct. The District Magistrate asked me to file my explanation.

In the statement which I submitted to the District Magistrate on August 14, 1925, I explained the circumstances justifying my comments in a bit stronger tone than that used in my original note published in the Ranbir. The last para of my statement read: "The Ranbir as organ of the best thoughts in the State, owed it to the public to give expression to the views which every well-wisher of the State held in the matter. The comment in the Ranbir, you will kindly see, was *bona fide* and made purely in the interest of the ruler and the people of the State." The District Magistrate felt amazed, if not embarrassed, and remarked "you are inviting more trouble." I submitted that my cause was just and that I was prepared to suffer the consequences. We both then had an informal meeting and after that I left the Court. After some days I came to know that the State Council had dropped the case against me. Later on, it transpired that the District Magistrate while returning my case to the Council, had also somewhere in his note "hinted" that the Editor had been told (of course, without my knowing anything about it) to be more careful in future in such matters. The District Magistrate had in his wisdom adopted this course obviously to save face of the Council. The whole episode enhanced the reputation of the Ranbir and it became a talk of the town.

I had another interesting encounter with another powerful Englishman, Mr. G.E.C. Wakefield, then Chief Secretary to Maharaja Hari Singh. One day I was discussing with him in his office chambers some important matters concerning the welfare of the people of the State and in that context, I asked him to request the Maharaja to take certain immediate steps in the public interest. As if to strike a bargain, Mr. Wakefield asked me in return to write an article on a particular subject and in this connection went so far as to even dictate the lines on which the article should be written. This appeared to me to be against all canons of journalism. I felt he was perhaps still thinking of himself as my boss (I had served as an accountant cum clerk in the Private Domains of Raja Hari Singh under Mr. Wakefield).

In a rather excited tone I told Mr. Wakefield that I had not come there to be advised by him as to what I should write or should not write in my paper: that should be left to the Editor's discretion. The shrewd Englishman noticing my chagrin at once replied that he never meant to dictate on me: he was simply making a suggestion which I might take up or reject: that was entirely my (Editor's) concern, he agreed. This smoothened me. Indeed, I felt within myself that I ought not to have addressed him in the way I did. Perhaps Editor in me, on the spur of the moment, got the better of me, Mr. Wakefield who later became the Foreign and Political Minister, did not, however, let the episode pass easily. Hardly two years after the event, when I went to him to know as to why the publication of the Ranbir had been banned, his terse reply was 'you were riding on elephant.'

There was one notorious *tehsildar* Raizada Ralia Ram. A case of wrongful confinement and extortion of money had been filed against him by one Sham Das Shah, resident of Doda, in the Session Court at Jammu. A departmental enquiry against the conduct of the *tehsildar* in the matter had already been held by Sheikh Abdul Qayum, Sub-division Magistrate Udhampur, under orders of the Revenue Minister, Major General Thakur Janak Singh. The Ranbir published the report verbatim as submitted by the Sub-Divisional Magistrate to the Revenue Minister. Almost the whole official world was up at arms against what they, in their wisdom, described as 'insolent and overbearing conduct' of the Editor of the Ranbir. On the complaint lodged by the *tehsildar*, the Revenue Minister sent for me to know the source of my information. As honour bound, I point-blank refused to divulge the source. Thereupon, the Revenue Minister threatened me with prosecution. My simple reply was 'come what may'. Ultimately the *tehsildar* filed a petition before the Session Judge complaining that by the publication in the Ranbir of the report of Sub-Divisional Magistrate the Editor had tried to prejudice the criminal proceedings pending against him in his court. The Session Judge, Dewan Bodh Raj Sawhney, was too shrewd to be taken in. He consigned the complaint to the office record.

Likewise a petition-writer filed a suit of defamation against me in the Court of City Magistrate, Jammu, complaining that the Ranbir had accused him of trafficking in women. The man had been actually found shuttling between Jammu and Bombay in suspicious circumstances. I had to undertake arduous journeys to far off places to produce solid evidence proving his nefarious activities. After a number of appearances before the Court, the case against me fell through.

Another case of similar nature was filed against me by one Lachman Singh on August 30, 1927, in the same court. It also met the same fate and I came out unscathed. I had, by quoting facts and figures in the Ranbir, accused Lachman Singh and his wife of working as agents on behalf of a gang abducting women and girls from Jammu and disposing them off in Bombay.

Once a Magistrate at first claimed from me damages of Rs. 5,000.00 and then withdrew his notice. He was late Sahibzada Mohd. Umar functioning as a Munsiff Magistrate at Samba - my hometown, in the year 1927. As a dramatist and litterateur, the Sahibzada enjoyed a great reputation, and I was on intimate and friendly terms with him. The public of Samba, however, had some grudge against the Magistrate in relation to his court work. The voice of the people in this respect naturally found a place in the hospitable columns of the Ranbir. Thereupon, a senior member of the Jammu bar, Sheikh Abdul Aziz, served me with a notice demanding on behalf of his client, Sahibzada Mohd. Umar, that I should pay as damages a sum of Rupees Five Thousand by way of compensation for the loss of his reputation resulting from the publication of comments against him in the Ranbir or be prepared to face prosecution in a court of law.

The receipt of this notice only steeled my heart and through the medium of my paper, I urged upon the State Government the need for immediately setting up of an impartial tribunal to enquire into the allegations against the magistrate after suspending or at least transferring him from Samba in the interest of administration. The magistrate immediately addressed a letter to me on *Karthik 12, 1984,* unconditionally withdrawing his notice and also informing me of his having withdrawn the application he had submitted to the Government seeking to permission to launch both civil and criminal proceedings against me. After some years, the magistrate gave up his service and lent weight of his pen to the literary columns of the Ranbir.

These few encounters will bring home to my readers the nature of difficulties that initially beset the first newspaper of the State in voicing out grievances of the people and in trying to bring out reformation in the social set-up. The receipt of personal and threats and minatory letters from persons who felt grieved by the writings in the Ranbir was a common feature those days. All this, however, kept me always on guard. Any act of indifference or complacency on my part in editing the paper would have proved ruinous.

The question before me was not merely to fill up the pages of the Ranbir but what was needed most and was done, was that all the material published in the Ranbir bore the stamp of authenticity. The result was that whatever appeared in the Ranbir came to be regarded as absolutely trustworthy. This greatly enhanced the reputation of the Ranbir and its Editor too.

The campaign that I persistently carried on in the Ranbir against the vilest social evil of the day, the Trafficking in women, and my successful emergence out of the court cases against me as narrated above, also earned for the Ranbir the title inter-alia prepared of a social reformer. When the State Government announced the appointment of a committee for the prevention of trafficking in women, I was appointed its member-secretary. Thakur Kartar Singh, then Governor of Jammu was the president of the Committee. As secretary of the Committee I inter-alia prepared a booklet entitled 'The Prevention of Trafficking in Women' underlining this social curse and the measures to supress it.

Suppression of infanticide, abolition of untouchability and the forced labour, prevention of infant marriage and juvenile smoking and removal of many other social evils formed chief plank of the Ranbir which can legitimately own credit for the enactment of various measures initiated during the regime of Maharaja Hari Singh in the field of social reforms.

# CHAPTER 6

# The White Man's Burden

I have mentioned earlier my encounter with Mr. Wakefield. He had since risen to the position of the Foreign and Political Minister of Maharaja Hari Singh who had succeeded to the throne after the demise of Maharaja Pratap Singh in 1925. Not only the general policy of the Ranbir but my growing contact with the freedom moment in India had turned Mr. Wakefield furious against me. Soon he got an opportunity to crush me.

In British India, Mahatma Gandhi, in pursuance of his civil disobedience movement, started the historic march to Dandi to break salt law on March 12, 1930. It created a great stir from one end of the country to the other which led to arrest of all prominent Congress leaders including Pandit Jawahar Lal Nehru, Maulana Abul Kalam Azad, Sardar Patel and Shri C. Rajagopalachari. The news of the arrest of Mahatma Gandhi spread like wild conflagration. There were hartals and processions throughout the country.

How could Jammu keep behind? There was a spontaneous hartal. The college and school students came out of their classrooms in thousands. All business establishments were completely closed. Hindus, Muslims, Sikhs and others including large number of ladies, took out processions parading the thoroughfares and shouting national slogans. The processionists also made bonfire of foreign clothes. A donkey with European hat on was the centre of special attention in these demonstrations. Mr. Wakefield who also held the portfolio of local self-government, summoned an extraordinary meeting of the Jammu Municipal Committee at his residence. When he was making a certain query from the Municipal commissioners, the president of the committee, Pandit Agya ram, rose to explain something whereupon Mr. Wakefield in an angry pose exclaimed; *"Ham yeh bakwas sun-na nahin chahte"* (I do not want to hear this nonsense). Pandit Agya Ram spiritedly retorted; "As the Minister has insulted me by the use of such words, I do not want to continue as the president of the Municipal Committee and hereby tender my resignation." Mr. Wakefield quipped, "Very well".

All these things, the unprecedented hartal and biggest ever demonstration in the history of Jammu, the procession of donkey with a European hat on, the bonfire of foreign clothes, the national slogans and last but not the least the insulting behaviour towards the civic chief were prominently published in the form of a special edition of the Ranbir. This upset Mr. Wakefield who had already felt much annoyed particularly at what had the previous day. He took a copy of the Ranbir with him, had a talk with the Resident in Kashmir, then hurried to the palace and held long consultations with Maharaja Hari Singh.

The result was the issuance of an order signed the Maharaja himself. The order dated May 9, 1930, read:

"My attention has been drawn to the account in the special issue of the Ranbir dated Baisakhi 25, Samvat 1987, corresponding to May 7, 1930, of the disgraceful demonstrations which lately took place in the city of Jammu in connection with the arrest in British India of Mr. Gandhi. The account in question not only gives unnecessary prominence to an affair with which my people have no concern but is highly malicious and grossly misleading so far as the intentions and policy of myself and my Government and conduct of the Police in relation to the demonstrations in question is concerned. The intensity of public feeling, the strength of the crowd assembled on the occasion, the number of women and school and college boys attending the demonstrations, the extent of the hartal and its so-called spontaneous character, have all been highly exaggerated. Not content with such wilful misrepresentations the account contains among other inaccuracies the following misstatements:

۱ ۔ سری مہاراجہ بہادر نے اپنے تدبر اور معاملہ فہمی سے حالات پر قابو پا لیا

۲ ۔ ہر جگہ یہی چرچا تھا کہ سری مہاراجہ بہادر نے ہدایات فرمائی ہیں کہ جلوس کو جہاں تک کہ وہ پرامن رہے کچھ بھی نہ کہا جائے ۔

۳ ۔ سنی انسپکٹر پولیس اور ایک سب انسپکٹر پولیس نے طلبا کے سامنے آ کر اور ان کے چند لیڈروں کو بلا کر کہا کہ اب جبکہ آپ کافی مظاہرہ کر چکے ہیں، انہیں منتشر ہو جانا چاہیے ۔

۴ ۔ طلبا شہر کے ہر حصے میں نعرے لگاتے اور مہاراجہ بہادر کی جے کے نعرے بلاتے تھے

۵ ۔ تمام فضا قومی نعروں سے گونج رہی تھی اور ساتھ ہی مہاراجہ بہادر کے جیکارے بلاتے جاتے تھے

More can be quoted but the above extracts will suffice to show that the whole meaning and implication of the account is to covey that I and my Government either actively promoted the demonstrations or at least connived at it or showed indifference as long as it was non-violent in character. It is unnecessary for me to repudiate such an allegation which carries its own refutation. I have all along held the views that it is not for me, my Government or my people to interfere in the affairs of British India and it has been a cordial article of faith with me to observe scrupulously my treaty obligations with the British Government according to practice of civilized Government. One of these obligations is not to countenance or permit any political demonstrations within my territory against the British Government. It has given me great pain to find the extracts to which I refer above violate this fundamental political principle. They also constitute flagrant breach of the undertaking given by the Editor and proprietor Lala Mulk Raj Saraf when permission was given by the State Council to him to start the Ranbir vide State council Resolution No. 8 dated March 18, 1924, I hereby direct that the permission accorded to the publication of the Ranbir be immediately cancelled and its further publication stopped.

"In issuing this order I desire to make it quite clear that it is not my intention to curb in any way the legitimate expression of opinion or fair and just criticism of the policy and acts of myself and my government. The policy regarding these matters will continue unchanged and I shall be quite willing to entertain application whether in Jammu or in Kashmir or both, from other journalists wishing to start another newspaper or newspapers within the State territory so long as their bona fide are not in question".

Sd/- Hari Singh<br>
Maharaja<br>
K.C.I.F., K.C.V.O.

Maharaja Hari Singh was generally known for his progressive and independent views. To have to pass an order of such a sweeping nature and in the way it had been done, could only reveal the inherent weakness of the Indian princes vis-à-vis the mighty British Empire. The Ranbir was not only the first newspaper of the Jammu and Kashmir State but also remained the only newspaper since its inception in 1924. The paper had done remarkably well during the few years it had been in existence as borne out by various unsolicited testimonials received from time to time from responsible quarters. Moreover, while publishing account of the Jammu demonstrations the Ranbir had only erred on the side of moderation. It had exercised due care to avoid any impression that the Ruler or the State Government had any hand whatsoever in the popular protest against Gandhiji's arrest. The British ingenuity, however, gave to the whole affair such a twist as made or perhaps compelled the Maharaja to feel as he did observe, "The whole meaning and implication of the account (as published in special issue of the Ranbir) is to convey that I and my Government either actively promoted the demonstration or at least connived at it or showed indifference so long it was non-violent in character. It is unnecessary for me to repudiate such an allegation which carries its own refutation."

In expressing tremendous public reaction to the arrest of Gandhiji, I little realised that I was needling the British Political Department on a delicate issue and in the process causing a strain in the relationship between the State of Jammu and Kashmir and the British Government. The Ranbir had the unique distinction of getting an order signed by the Ruler himself in which detailed reasons for immediately cancelling the permission accorded to the publication of the Paper, were stated and the treaty rights of the suzerain Power visa-vis Princely States quoted chapter verse so much that the Maharaja pleaded:

"I have all along held the view that it is not for me, my Government or my people to interfere in the affairs of British India and it has been a cordial article of faith with me to observe scrupulously my treaty obligations with the British Government according to practices of civilized government. One of these obligations is not to countenance or permit any political demonstrations within my territory against the British Government. It has given me great pain to find the extracts to which I refer above violate this fundamental political principle." The order was obviously more an explanation to the Political Department than a fiat against a humble Paper.

The Ranbir was thus sacrificed at the altar of political exigency. I was personally made a special target in as much as the royal order laid down that I alone could not apply to start another newspaper.

The question of breach of any conditions did not at all arise. No conditions whatsoever were attached with the Council Resolution No 8 dated March 18, 1924 which, as conveyed to me merely read: "His Highness the Maharaja Bahadur in Council has been pleased to accord permission under section 5 of the Jammu and Kashmir Press and Publications Regulations 1971 to a paper being started by Lala Mulk Raj Saraf B.A."

In the beginning I did make some representations to the Maharaja for reconsideration of his order but it did not evoke any response whatsoever. Each time I met Mr. Wakefield in this connection, I was shown cold shoulder.

I was, however, determined to have a newspaper on my own. Pandit Ganga Nath Sharma and Lala Shiv Ram Gupta had already worked with me as the joint-editor and Manager of the Ranbir. We three planned to start a newspaper from Lahore. We named it as 'Amar'. Though printed and published at Lahore, it was edited and distributed in Jammu and Kashmir State like the Ranbir. Later on, Pandit Ganga Nath Sharma and myself parted company with Mr. Gupta leaving him in sole charge of the Amar. Immediately afterwards we both in collaboration with two colleagues Shri Vishwa Nath Wadehra, formerly manager of the Ranbir and Shri Krishan Smailpuri, the well-known Dogri poet, started another paper, the Mashir just like Amar. The Mashir continued to appear till the resuscitation of the Ranbir in November 1931. It is noteworthy that notwithstanding the clear desire of the Maharaja, as expressed in the order banning the publication of the Ranbir, to entertain application from journalists other than myself to start another newspaper or newspapers, no paper came to be published within the State territory and the only newspaper that was permitted to appear after the lapse of more than 18 months was again the Ranbir.

The period extending over to 18 months (May 9, 1930 to November 13, 1931) was indeed most crucial in the modern history of Jammu and Kashmir. It witnessed many an upheaval. There were communal clashes in the State. Hundreds of people had been behind the bars. The *Ahrars* of the Punjab who called themselves nationalist Muslims had begun to pour in the State to participate in a civil disobedience movement with a view to assisting their agitating co-religionists. As soon as the *Ahrars* entered the State territory at Suchetgarh, the border town on old Jammu Sialkot road, they were placed under arrest. The number of such arrests swelled to many thousands and five thousand of those arrested had to be consigned to the Punjab. The reaction of non-Muslims to the Muslim agitation was quite baneful. Mistakes were being committed on all sides. The Muslims in their fanaticism, thought of the State Government as a Hindu Government and hence were not prepared to give it credit even if it did anything right or proper. The Hindus in their foolishness regarded every agitation by Muslims, even if it meant to benefit the whole population, as anti-Hindu and hence they were led, rather misled, to almost invariably side with the Government however erring. The seed of communalism thus got deep-rooted. There was, in fact, utter lack of that sobering influence which the presence of the Ranbir and its national outlook used to carry. Soon a sense of realism began to dawn on the powers that be. Mr. Wakefield ad to leave the State unhonoured, unwept and unsung. Raja Hari Kishan Koul took over as the Prime Minister of the State. He tried to pacify various sections of the people. Several changes were announced in the administrative set-up of the State. The majority of Muslims, however, continued to rumble. Compelled by the force of circumstances, the State Government in their wisdom thought of reviving the Ranbir. While I was busy as usual, in my office conducting the affairs of the Mashir, I got a telegram from the Prime Minister himself from Srinagar on November 13, 1931, corresponding to *Kartik* 28, 1988, which read "Orders issued Governor regarding restarting Ranbir".

The order for the revival of the Ranbir was, in fact, as sudden and surprising as it was the order for the closing down on May 9, 1930. The State Government appeared to feel much relieved over the reappearance of the Ranbir as indicated by an official statement published in the Statesman of December 1, 1931. It said: "As official of Kashmir State who is in Delhi with the Prime Minister who is in Delhi with the Prime Minister Raja Hari Kishan Koul yesterday informed a Statesman representative that the ban on the publication of newspaper in the State has been lifted to the extent of permitting the reissue of the Ranbir published weekly in Jammu". I was flooded with messages of congratulations and felicitations on the removal of the ban.

As I had continued to be active in journalism, it did not take me long to bring out the Ranbir anew. During a and a half, the period covered by the suspension of the Ranbir, two notable developments took place. The State Government, in April 1931, chose to utilise my services in connection with the proposed establishment of the Jammu and Kashmir Bank. The State Finance Minister, Mr. P.K. Wattal, under his letter No.261-C dated April 25, 1931 wrote to me: "His Highness' Government has been pleased to nominate you as a Joint-Secretary of the Central Committee for carrying on the work of publicity and educative propaganda and for the collection of share applications of the Jammu and Kashmir Bank which is to be established shortly."

Taking it as a work of public utility, I gave my consent and began to work in right earnestness in association with Major General Dewan Bishan Das, formerly Prime Minister of the State, who was appointed as the Chairman of the Central Committee, and Wazir Tej Ram the General Treasurer, who was made the Secretary. On May 26, 1931, I was informed that "an allowance of Rs. 150/- per month had been sanctioned in your favour as the Joint Secretary." This set me athinking. I felt it derogatory to accept any renumeration from the Government for such a social service as it appeared to me. I, therefore, declined to accept any pay and volunteered to work in an honorary capacity. The Finance Minister wrote back to me under his office No. 361-C dated May 16, 1931 "I am glad to learn from the proceedings of the Central Committee that you have volunteered to serve as Joint Secretary without any renumeration and thank you for the public spirit you have shown in the matter."

Later, Colonel E.J.D. Colvin, the new Prime Minister, under his D.O, No. 10383 dated 5.10.1932 said "I have much pleasure in placing on record my appreciation of the good work done by you in connection with the establishment of the State Bank and especially your public spirit in volunteering your services as Joint Secretary in an honorary capacity.

In September 1931, I had been elected as the President of the All-India Mahajan Conference, succeeding Lal Mehar Chand Mahajan who became Chief Justice of India after Independence.

In my presidential address delivered at the 16th Annual Session of the All-India Mahajan Conference held on October 14-19, 1931, at Shakargarh (now in West Pakistan) I *inter alia* stressed the role of the press in moulding public opinion in favour of social reforms. The Tribune, Lahore, reported on October 20, 1931: "Two thousand delegates and others attended the 16th All India Mahajan conference which was presided over by Lala Mulk Raj Saraf, Editor of the Jammu Ranbir. His presidential address contained suggestions regarding the all-round betterment of the Mahajan community as an important part of the Indian nation."

The Ranbir re-appeared in November 1931. I was still the only newspaper in the State. In the years to come I had to take part in numerous public activities some of which will be briefly mentioned in the following pages under appropriate chapters.

# CHAPTER 7

# The Rattan

The Rattan was a child of the Ranbir. The year 1934 saw several newspapers and periodicals coming out in the State. This was mostly due to the relaxation of the State Press Law. All these journals, however, were meant for the adolescent and generally dealt with local socio-economic problems. There was no magazine for the children which in fast changing world appeared to me an imperative need of the hour. As a parent and lover of the young, I felt an urge to bring out one. This was the nucleus of the monthly Rattan which made its appearance in December, 1934. Fortunately, it soon acquired an all-India reputation and came to be regarded as one of the three best edited children's magazines in the country.

Mr. Shanti Sarup Nishat (now Dr. S.S. Nishat, Kashmir Trade Agent in Bombay), one of the assistant editors of the Ranbir and both a poet and a writer, was the first Editor of the Rattan with myself as its printer, publisher and director. Two years later my eldest son Om who was still a high school student, took over the control of the Rattan. In later years when Om, free from University education became an active associate with ne in the Ranbir, one of his talented friends Mr. Kundan Lal, a highly educated and competent young man who is now a Professor in the Delhi University assumed the editorship of the Rattan. These young intellectuals well versed as they were in the art of writing for children, were able in due course of time, to enlist co-operation of some eminent writers and specialists in children's literature in the country. All this had tremendously added to the popularity of the Rattan in mid 1940s.

As newsprint was a rationed article in those days and could not be secured in the State without the previous consent of the Resident in Kashmir, it became difficult for us to cope with the vastly increasing circulation of the Rattan. In this connection an extract from the letter No. D=7 (P) 45 dated December 8, 1945, from the Director of Civil Supplies, Jammu and Kashmir Government to the Extra-Assistant to Resident in Kashmir is worth mentioning: "The conductors of the Rattan have made a demand for an additional quota of 200 reams a month on account of its increased circulation which is verified and certified to be 25,000 copies. The educational authorities of those States and British India Provinces where Urdu is spoken, have placed the journal on approved lists/ Throughout India, he demand for its copies is, therefore, increasing and a fairly large number of orders, have been by the management from individual subscribers and institutions from such distant places as Kapurthala, Rampur, Hyderabad, Bhopal, U.P., C.P., Berar, Sidh and even in Bombay and Madras. His Highness's Government are, therefore, satisfied that the demand of increase in paper ration of the journal is genuine and justified and therefore, strongly recommend that on the basis of the certified number of copies in circulation and the demand still continuing, the newsprint ration of the Rattan be increased to 160 reams a month." The Rattan, in fact, had its subscribers even in several Asian and African countries where Urdu-knowing Indians lived.

The annual illustrated special edition of the Rattan "Karan Number" named after Yuvraj (now Maharaja) Karan Singh used to be a unique feature of the Rattan. It provided a great literary treat from year to year. I am told that the presentation copies of the Karan Number continue to adorn the shelf of the rich library owned by the Governor Dr. Karan Singh. On seeing the Annual Number of the Rattan, that eminent Urdu poet and litterateur Pandit Brij Mohan Dattatraya Kaifi in his letter dated Model Town, Lahore, the 14th April 1937, wrote: "Good God, the material that has been collected for the Number and the excellent way it has got up is highly commendable. Perhaps the people are not unaware that you are the founder of journalism in Jammu and Kashmir State. Just as your well-known paper, the Rattan is unique and unsurpassable as the first magazine of the children. I wonder whether to prefer your first production Ranbir to the second one or second to the first one. Not only the public of Jammu and Kashmir but the whole Urdu world should be grateful to you."

Prime Minister Col. Colvin observed on February 23, 1937: "Mr. Mulk Raj Saraf is the Editor of the Ranbir, Jammu, the oldest paper in the State. He has conducted the paper in a responsible manner and has on the whole steered clear of communalism. He is also the director of a beautiful got-up children's magazine entitled the Rattan which brings out an excellent special number on the birthday of Shri Yuvraj Bahadur.

"Mr. Saraf's outlook is liberal and he appears to have properly understood the true responsibility of a journalist and public man. I hope he will continue to maintain the good traditions that he has as a publicist built for himself. I think that he is serving the State and the people in commendable manner."

Shri Gopalswamy Aiyengar who was he Prime Minister of the State during the second world war in his message on March 18, 1943, observed: "The Rattan's special numbers have been widely appreciated both in the State and outside. It has always maintained a good standard and has provided informing matter of a varied nature particularly of vale to the children. Educational effort in the State has been and is making rapid progress and the service which journals like the Rattan contribute in this cause is always welcome."

Mr. Wajahat Hussain I.C.S., Home and Education Minister, wrote on March2, 1937 "Rattan is the most popular and useful magazine. I have been its regular subscriber since its birth. Its articles have been contributed by a number of eminent men in the world of Urdu literature and I have always been impressed by the high tones of these articles."

Shri B.N. Rau, Prime Minister who later became the Constitutional Adviser to the Government of India, in his message on March 16, 1944, said: "Today is the birthday of Shri Yuvraj Bahadur and is a day of general rejoicing. He is still in his boyhood and he lives the life of an ordinary school boy, claiming none of the privileges of his rank. ,It is, therefore, natural that he has come to be regarded as a symbol of the youth of the State and, following a kindly custom, I now send this message of good wishes to all the young boys and girls of the State, as if his birthday was also their."

Once I made request to Maharaja Hari Singh to ask the Yuvraj to send a message in his own hand for the Karan Number of the Rattan. In reply Col. Dr, Shri Kailash Narayan Haksar who was tutor to Yuvraj Bahadur and also personal adviser to Maharaja sent me a letter in Urdu dated January 20, saying, "His Highness has commanded that in view of his being very young, it would not be proper to publish a message, however, brief, from the Yuvraj. Moreover, he should not be made to feel that he had acquired a status and rank that every word coming from him was like a sermon to the masses."

Unfortunately, the partition dislocated the arrangements for the publication of the Rattan. The services of some of its artists and calligraphists based in Lahore were no more available. The Rattan made its last appearance in September, 1947, when it was at its height of glory. Even after the lapse of nearly 20 years now hardly a week passes without an order or two being received by me from some part of India or Pakistan for the supply of Rattan. An attempt was made to revive the Rattan in the form of a Hindi magazine monthly in 1965. It was published for a few months under the editorship of my eldest grandson, Subhash. But for various reasons the attempt had to be given up.

In mid-1950's two new magazines were started by me, one Monthly "THE KASHMIR INDUSTRY" and other a socio-tourist Weekly "THIS WEEK IN KASHMIR". The working editor of the K.I. was my eldest son, Om Saraf and that of T.W.I.K. was my youngest son, Sat Saraf who later joined the Hindustan Times and is at present working as its Deputy Chief Reporter in New Delhi. Both the periodicals, however, did not last long and had to be stopped for lack of sufficient funds.

# CHAPTER 8

# As a Printer

When the Ranbir took birth in 1924, there was no private printing press in Jammu. I had to setup the one. As indicated earlier the permission to start the paper included the permission to start a printing press. With extremely meagre resources at my disposal, I could hardly afford to establish a power-driven plant. It was, therefore, decided to have a hand-driven litho press for which the skilled labour was employed on piece-work basis from the local Government Press. It was only in 1932, sometimes after re-appearance of the Ranbir, that a foreign made electric printing machine along with an experienced machine man Pandit Balak Nath, was imported from Lahore. By then a few more local papers had come into being and the financial position of the Ranbir had somewhat improved. The District Magistrate of Jammu, Colonel Baldev Singh Pathania, inspected the Public Printing Press as it was named, on November 3, 1934 and *inter alia* observed: "About a dozen men are employed on different duties in this Press. Almost all the Urdu newspapers of Jammu are printed here. It is a great effort on the part of Lala Mulk Raj Saraf who has vast experience having worked in various capacities in the public. With such a man as the proprietor, it is going to be a grand show in due course."

The power-driven machine indeed proved a great boost for the newspapers from Jammu as well as Mirpur and Poonch. As a printer I was automatically made responsible for the maintenance of certain standards of the printed word not only in my own paper but also all other newspapers printed at my press. Not infrequently, I had to pay the price for being a printer whenever the Ranbir or any other paper printed at my press was victimised. At times, I had to suffer for the printing of other material also such as the posters and pamphlets which began to be published with growing public activity. With the passage of time, my printing concern did become a grand show. I bought several other machines in 1940's all of which, however, were disposed off in 1950's. It will not be out of place to recollect here some of the memorable experiences in my capacity as the keeper of a printing press.

The Inkishaf Jammu of January 20, 1936, printed at my press, published an article captioned "Rajputs do not require Rao Bahadur Thakur Kartar Singh: they want Wazir Zorawar Singh." Rao Bahadur was the Finance Minister at that time and the Wazir was the famous Dogra General who conquered Ladakh more than 100 years ago. This was taken by the State Government as 'an attack on a minister in his ministerial capacity likely to bring the Government of His Highness the Maharaja Bahadur into contempt.' A letter from one Thakur Kashmiri Lal Parihar of Kishtwar published in the same issue of the paper was also considered by the Government as 'likely to bring into hatred or contempt Rajputs, a class of His Highness subjects.' Another article against Rao Bahadur Thakur Kartar Singh in the issue of the Inkishaf of January 27, 1936, was regarded by the Government as 'likely to bring into hatred or contempt the Government established by law in the State by holding up to ridicule one of the ministers.'

All these articles were considered by the Government objectionable as 'violating the provisions of section 19, sub-section (1) of the Jammu and Kashmir Press and Publications Regulation No. 1 of Samvat 1989'. On February 20, 1936, I, as the keeper of the Press where the Inkshaf was printed, was served with a notice by the officiating Prime Minister, Sir Barjor Dalal, to make a deposit of Rs. 500.00 in cash, before March 9, 1936, in the office of the District Magistrate, Jammu, otherwise the consequences of failure to deposit security under section 20 of the Press regulation will follow'.

I deposited the amount under protest. On June 4, 1936, Prime Minister Colvin cancelled the earlier order and refunded my deposit.

In 1937, there was a cow-agitation in Jammu when the contempt of court proceedings were initiated against me. This was a sequel to the printing of a poster at my press announcing the holding of public meeting by the Hindu Sikh Naujawan Sabha to protest against the State High Court decision reducing the sentence of three accused persons in a cow-slaughter case. The legality of the poster was definitely chargeable. In fact, the poster had got printed in my absence from the town. But then a mass agitation followed. I was externed from the town as a press correspondent. The agitation came to an end after 35 days of hartal in Jammu. Consequently, the contempt proceedings against me were also dropped.

In late 1940's when my relations were unfortunately somewhat strained with the then Prime Minister, Sheikh Abdullah, and the Ranbir was soon to cease publication, the text-book business had been nationalised. The service of all the private presses were requisitioned to ensure prompt publication of the manuscripts. Mine being the foremost printing press of the State, was also allocated a portion of the task after necessary formalities had been completed. But hardly half of the job was done, when it appeared to a lieutenant of the Sheikh that I was perhaps being unduly patronised. Mr. J.N. Sharma, the head of the printing department, visited me at my residence and apprised me of his predicament in face of the instructions he had received from the above. I immediately asked my manager to deliver back the authorities the undone part of the assignment.

The Kashmir Constituent Assembly came into being in November 1951. While the representatives of the people had thus become sovereign, the new constitution could be given to the people of the State only on January 26, 1956. In between as a keeper of the press, I had to wage and lose my last battle. The Kashmir Mail – a local Urdu weekly edited by Bakshi Bodh Raj Manawari, a gentleman of great integrity, and printed in my press, had published an article which Shekh Abulla's Cabinet considered derogatory to their regime. I was ordered to deposit with the District Magistrate, Jammu a security of Rs. 1000.00. Considering this to be tune with the spirit of the times, I approached the State High Court for setting aside the Cabinet order. The full bench of the High Court dismissed my prayer, *inter alia*, observing: "There is no doubt that the right of freedom of discussion and the liberty of the press are fundamental doctrines of democracy.........But at the same time the court has to construe the Act as it is. The Court is bound to give effect to the language of the Act so long as it is in existence even though it thinks that the provisions of the Act have not kept pace with the changed time."

I, however, did not deposit the security demanded. Instead, I decided to dispose off all my printing machines. After the disappearance of the Ranbir in 1950, my interest in them as a mere commercial concern was on the wane. By about late 1950's, I had all my stores auctioned. This enabled me to devote my single-minded attention to journalism as a newsman.

# CHAPTER 9

# The Ranbir at 18 and Later

The Ranbir completed its eighteenth year of service on June 2, 1942. It was indeed an occasion of great joy for all of those associated with the birth and growth of the first newspaper in the State. Naturally I was the recipient of numerous messages of greetings from the friends including prominent brother journalists and other public men belonging to different shades of opinion in and outside Jammu and Kashmir. There could be no greater acknowledgement of the impartiality with which the Ranbir had been presenting 'the sacred facts' to its readers. I also felt inclined to construe such wide-spread appreciation as an ample measure of success the Ranbir had achieved in offering its free comment with malice towards none in regard to the various complex problems facing the people of the State. Reproduced below are the extracts from many congratulatory messages on the attainment of adolescence by the Ranbir.

**Maulana Zafar Ali Editor the Zamindar Lahore and a member of the Central Legislative Council:** Because of its impartial views and harmonious outlook, the Ranbir is popular amongst all sections of people of Jammu and Kashmir. Lala Mulk Raj Saraf deserves much praise that amidst many difficulties and obstacles for the truth speaking newsmen in the Indian States, he has been successfully conducting himself as an editor.

**Mahashay Krishan Editor of the Daily Pratap Lahore:** I have known Lala Mulk Raj Saraf for a considerable period of time. He is an able and experienced newspaperman. I have nothing but praise for the way he has crossed over hurdles and made his paper a success. The Ranbir has indeed played a conspicuous part in the present awakening in the State.

**Shri Ranbir Chief Editor the Daily Milap Lahore:** Lala Mulk Raj Saraf can feel well proud of the services of the Ranbir rendered to the people of the Jammu and Kashmir State for the last eighteen years. God has granted him resolute head and a determined heart; hence he has been able to brave all difficulties in order to serve the people.

**Pandit Mela Ram Wafa Editor the Vir Bharat Lahore:** I know Lala Mulk Raj Saraf from the time we used to work in the daily Bande Matram started by late lamented Lala Lajpat Rai. Shri Saraf possesses keen intellect and congenial disposition and is an independent newspaper man. Both my esteemed friend and the Ranbir have contributed a great deal in the all-round awakening that we find in Jammu and Kashmir today. The Ranbir can also rightly claim to have set up a high standard of journalism in this part of the country.

**Munshi Mohd Din Fauq Editor the Kashmiri Magazine Lahore:** The Ranbir has suffered for its independent thinking. Both the Government and the people feel the impact of its writings.

**Pandit Prem Nath Kamnath Editor the Daily Martand Srinagar:** It is our good fortune that we have a journalist of the standing of Lala Mulk Raj Saraf amidst us. He is above regional prejudices and is a true nationalist. The Ranbir has always stood rock-like against the adversaries.

**Mr. J.N. Zutshi Editor the Kashmir Sentinel Srinagar:** It is extremely difficult to beat the distinct record set up by the Ranbir in the service of the people during the last eighteen years.

**Pandit Prem Nath Bazaz Editor the Hamdard Srinagar:** These past eighteen years that the Ranbir has been in existence, have witnessed a great political upheaval in Jammu and Kashmir. The Ranbir can rightly feel proud of being the first newspaper of the State. I feel no hesitation in asserting that the Ranbir by its efforts in the cause of the country has contributed its due share in making the State progress so far. Its inoffensive policy, the non-communal approach and consistency are commendable.

**Pandit Kashap Bandhu Editor the Desh Srinagar:** The journalism in Jammu and Kashmir not only started with the Ranbir, but it also took strides because of the Ranbir and every newspaperman should feel proud of what the Ranbir has been able to achieve.

**Pandit Dina Nath Mast Kashmiri Editor of the Rahbar Srinagar:** I always look upon Lala Mulk Raj Saraf as Lord Northcliff Jammu and Kashmir State. Even the worst detractors of Mr. Saraf admit the spirit of enterprise and determination with which he has guided the destinies of the Ranbir.

**Lala Hans Raj Mahajan Vakil, a great Social Reformer:** The role the Ranbir has played in the political awakening amongst the people of Jammu and Kashmir State, is unrivalled. Its popularity is based on its true nationalistic approach and its solid and useful writings. The attractive getup of the Ranbir and its regularity have become proverbial. For its treatment of various subjects, the Ranbir stands ahead of even some best-known newspapers of the Punjab. There is hardly any matter of public importance which the Ranbir does not reflect.

**Pandit Prem Nath Dogra (presently State Jana Sangh Chief):** June 24 is the red letter day in the annals of Jammu and Kashmir. It was on this day eighteen years ago that the first newspaper of Jammu and Kashmir came into existence. From its very inception the Ranbir has been a great supporter of the rights of the people irrespective of religion, caste or region. Perhaps few people are aware that for the sake of journalism Lala Mulk Raj Saraf, an old graduate voluntarily gave up a Government job. This spirit of sacrifice and selflessness has brought the Ranbir in the forefront of the best newspaper in the country.

**Mr. D.P. Dhar, President All-Kashmir Students' Conference (presently a minister in the State Cabinet):** The Ranbir is the outcome of brave and incessant efforts on the part of out of distinguished journalist, Lala Mulk Raj Saraf. The Ranbir has always maintained the highest tradition of journalism.

**Choudhry Ghulam Abbas President All Jammu and Kashmir Muslim Conference:** For a paper to continue to serve the people to the best of its ability for such a long time, is in itself a matter of great satisfaction. This is mainly due to the deep understanding, peaceful disposition and non-communal outlook of Lala Mulk Raj Saraf. One happy feature of the Ranbir from the public point of view is that it considers as its journalistic duty to criticise the Government whenever there is need for it.

**Wazir Ganga Ram, the Opposition Leader in the Legislative Assembly:** I personally know with what pleasurable inclination Maharaja Pratap Singh used to get the Ranbir read out to him regularly. I feel the greatest satisfaction and happiness in the fact that Lala Mulk Raj Saraf has conducted his paper in a very commendable manner and with perfect dignity.

**Major-General Samunder Khan Bahadur, Srinagar:** I am a regular reader of the Ranbir. It has fought and won many a battle in the field of social reforms. Its merit lies in the fact that it has stirred clear of communalism.

**Khan Sahib Mirza Ghulam Mustafa Landlord, Srinagar:** I have seen many newspapers come and gone like bubbles of water but the Ranbir continues to live because of its intrinsic worthy and praiseworthy policy. It not only lives but also flourishing and progressing and is looked upon with great esteem by every section of the people.

**Sardar Mool Singh Kosala, Retired Secretary:** I am an old and regular subscriber of the Ranbir. The determined manner in which Lala Mulk Raj Saraf has nurtured this plant is commendable.

**Khwaja Ghulam-ul-Saiyidain Director Education Jammu and Kashmir State:** The Ranbir belongs to the category of newspapers that are meant to serve the society. To add to the informative knowledge of the people and to diffuse true ideas to the public. Only such papers can guide the masses to distinguish between right and wrong.

**Dr. Mohd. Din Taseer Principal Amar Singh Degree College:** As a literary man I can positively assert that the language used by the Ranbir is not wrong and the manner of its writing is attractive and I always read it with zeal and flavour.

It may be mentioned here that from January 27, 1941, I experimented with the publication of the last page of the Ranbir in Hindi to cater to the Hindi knowing people. But it was a matter of regret that except for a letter of appreciation from Pandit Amar Nath Kak Advocate, then deputy President of the State Assembly, there was little public enthusiasm and the Hindi supplement had to be given up after a few weeks.

From August 30, 1943, the Ranbir began to be published twice a week. This proved a tremendous success and I was soon encouraged to seek permission to convert it into a daily but the authorities would not agree presumably in view of great tension that prevailed at that time all over the country as a result of full-scale clash between resurgent nationalist forces and foreign rule. It was only December 1, 1946, when the shape of things to come had become sufficiently clear at the national level that the Ranbir was allowed to appear as a daily.

1946 was also the year which marked the centenary of the Amritsar treaty between the British East India Company and Maharaja Gulab Singh. The treaty laid the foundation of modern State of Jammu and Kashmir. The

Ranbir, on this occasion issued a voluminous special issue title "Jammu and Kashmir Encyclopaedia" which has been recognised as a document of great historical importance. The following message by Maharaja Hari Singh adorned the opening page of Encyclopaedia: "A hundred years ago, my great grand-father Shri Maharaja Gulab Singh Ji founded the Jammu and Kasmir State, thereby bringing about the consolidation of the contagious territories of Jammu, Kasmir, Ladakh, Gilgit etc. to their lasting benefit. To commemorate the centenary of that historic event Lala Mulk Raj Saraf has undertaken the publication of the present volume which, I feel sure, will be of interest to readers within and without the State, I commend Lala Mulk Raj Saraf's enterprise and wish it all success."

# CHAPTER 10

## All State Editors' Meet

With the growth of journalism and increase in the number of newspapers and other periodicals that came to be published in the State, the question of getting together naturally began to interest their editors. At first an All–Jammu and Kashmir Journalists Association was formed in Jammu and myself as its President. It had its branch in Srinagar also. After some time there sprang up two regional bodies, one in Jammu with the old label and other in Srinagar named the Kashmir Newspapers' Society. On June 30, 1943, the Society entertained Shri P.T. Chandra, Editor the Tribune, and Mr. Shiva Rao, the New Delhi representative of the Hindu and the Manchester Guardian. Besides the editors of the local papers, prominent public men including Sheikh Abdullah and Pandit Jia Lal Kilam were also present. I also happened to be there. It was on this occasion that the idea of holding a session of All Jammu and Kashmir Newspaper Editors' Conference was mooted. On my return to Jammu I discussed the matter with the local colleagues and they all agreed with their Kashmir friends. Accordingly, on July 7, 1943, at a meeting sponsored by the Kashmir Newspapers' Society under the presidentship of Khwaja Sadar-ud-Din Mujahid, Editor the Khalid, a reception committee was formed. Pandit Prem Nath Kannah, Editor the Martand, was elected the Chairman Mr. Mujahid and Pandit Gwasha Lal Koul, Editor the Kashmir Chronicle, as the Vice-Presidents, Mr. J.N. Wali, Editor the Kashmir Times, as the General Secretary, Sardar Raghbir Singh Mukt, Editor the Shamsher, as the Secretary, Pandit Shambhu Nath Koul Nazir, Editor the Vakil, as the Publicity Secretary, Sardar Gurparb Singh, Editor the Khalsa Gazette, as the General Treasurer and Khwaja Ghulam Rasool Arif, Editor the Khidamat, as the Accountant. Several sub-committees were also setup.

A sum of rupees one thousand was collected on the spot. It was also decided at the meeting to invite Mr. Tushar Kanti Ghosh, Editor the Amrit Bazar Patrika, to inaugurate the conference. Later, the reception committee in consultation with the Jammu Journalists asked me to preside over the deliberations of the 3-day conference which was scheduled to commence in Srinagar on August 19, 1943.

At a meeting held in Jammu on July 16, 1943, under the presidentship of Pandit Vishwa Nath Kerni, Editor the Sudarshan, the local journalists resolved to make Srinagar conference a complete success. There was great enthusiasm among them and they also decided to hold the All-State Conference in Jammu and bear all the expenses in case it was not possible to hold the session of Srinagar due to the imposition of section 144 Cr. P.C. there. A subcommittee was setup to draft resolution to be put before the session.

A grand welcome was given at Jammu by the local journalists to Shri Tushar Kanti Ghosh on his arrival by train from Calcutta on the morning of august 19, 1943. After a brief stay in Jammu, Mr. Ghosh accompanied by the president-elect besides Pandit Vishwa Nath Kerni, Mr. Balraj Puri, editor the Pukar, Chowdhry Mohd. Shafi, Joint Editor the Sudarshan, Raizada Ajudhia Nath Vaid, Editor the Usha, and Kaviraj Vaishnu Gupta, Editor the Desh Sewak, left for Srinagar. At Qazi Gund Mr. Ghosh and the party were warmly received on behalf of the Reception Committee, by Sarvashri Mujahid, Wali, Shambhu Nath Koul, Gurparb Singh and Kanshi Nath Aima. Qazi Gund had been tastefully decorated. People had come even from adjoining villages to cheer the visiting newsmen. After tea at the dak bungalow, the party proceeded to Srinagar where thousands of people had assembled in the Lal Chowk (Red-square) to receive them. Those present included besides the local journalists, member of the Praja Sabha (the State Assembly), leaders of the various political social bodies and other distinguished gentry. At Hazuri Bagh where a big decorated pandal had been put up, Mr. Gopal Das Mengi, Joint Editor of the Sewak, Lala Girdhari Lal Anand, Editor the Anand, Khawaja Ghulam Qadir Bandey, representative of the Prabhat Poonch, Comrades Trilok Chand, Joint-Editor of the Sach, Mirpur, Mr. Dharam Vir, representative of the Sadaqat, Mirpur, Seth Shakuntla Chief Editor of the Usha, Kumari Sushila Tuli of the Usha, Sardar Mohinder Singh, Editor the Watan, Pandit Girdhari Lal Dogra, Honorary Editor the Kisan, and Mr. S.S. Nishat of the Hamdard.

A few journalists from the Punjab also attended the session as fraternal delegates. These, Editor included Mr. Hamid, Editor the Eastern Times, Lahore, Mr. Gian Chand Kanwal, Editor the Massihai-Jadid, and the President of the Christian Editors' Conference, Lahore, and Mr. P.D. Saggi – a freelance.

The plenary session of the conference was inaugurated on August 20, 1943, by Shi Tushar Kanti Ghosh. He felt proud to have come in touch with newspapermen in Jammu and Kashmir. This reminded him, he said, of 'old ties with Kashmir'. The reference pertained to the sensational disclosures made by the Amrit Bazar Patrika in 1885 regarding British conspiracy to dethrone Maharaja Pratap Singh. Pandit Prem Nath Kannah in his welcome address stressed the role that the newspapers could bring about all-round development in the country. He said, "It is our good fortune that a newspaper editor of the standing of Shri Mulk Raj Saraf with over a quarter of a century's experience in journalism at his back, has accepted to lead the all Jammu and Kashmir Newspaper Editors' Conference."

In my Presidential Address, I said *inter alia*:

"As I stand here today my thoughts are irresistibly turned to the journalism in the State, which, like an infant, is yet in its swaddling clothes and is passing through transitional stages. As such, it is needless to point out the comparatively speaking, journalism in the State falls short of the required standard of the talent, prestige and perfection – traits which have invariably characterised the journalism in British India. But we need not be sorry on that account as you know childhood is imperceptibly followed by youth as day follows the night. We are really optimistic about the great progress made by the journalism in the State in the brief history of its existence despite unfavourable circumstances and extreme difficulties with which it is beset. This incidentally provides us with a proof positive that the State journalists are alive to the responsibilities which are lodged on their shoulders.

"Journalism is undoubtedly an exciting and arduous mission whose scope is not merely confined to the publication of the news. Its horizon is wide and a true journalist would be failing in his duty if he does not make a dispassionate study of day-to-day events in right perspective, offer fearless comments couched in decent and appropriate language on the political, economic, cultural, social and other aspects of the life. Apparently, it seems to be quite easy but really speaking its completion revolves hard labour, well balanced judgement of business. What is a newspaper? An echo of the public voice. And what is the public voice? Nothing but the voice of the truth, vox populi vox Dei-the voice of the people is the voice of God. A journalist who hesitates in raising his voice for upholding truth and justice cannot deserve the honour of being called an editor, he is just like Begger who uses his paper as beggars' bowl.

"Long before the advent of journalism when monarchical and oligarchical forms of Government were prevalent, rulers many a time went out in disguise to keep themselves in touch with the public opinion. Gradually this primitive way of gathering information developed into full-fledged journalism based on organised and scientific lines. And today as you all know, press in a mighty power-'the fourth estate of the realm' I cannot do better than quote Sir John Browning who has aptly expressed as to how journalism exercises a healthy influence on all walks of life:

*But mightiest of the mighty means, on which the arm the arm of progress leans,*
*Man's noblest mission to advance*
*His woes assuage, his weal enhance*
*His rights enforce, his wrongs redress-*
*Mightiest of mighty is the press.*

"So far as the primary duty of an editor i.e. the publication of news is concerned, he has to discharge it honestly and whole-heartedly. He has to cater for almost of all the shades of interest and taste of his readers and not limit it exclusively to his personal choice. In the publication of news, he has bear in mind that they are based on true facts. One true news is worth more than hundreds of false and baseless rumours. Another guiding principle of true journalism is that a newspaper should in no case be made an instrument for grinding one's own axe. An editor should see that his very personality is lost in the glorification of high ideals. The tenets of journalism go so far as to require of him to invariably merge the first-person singular 'I' into plural 'we'. He should act as a mirror to the public opinion losing his identity in it. So far as the creation and formation of public opinion is concerned, the duty of an editor is all the more difficult. Sometimes he shall have to make great sacrifices in order to surmount hardships and obstacles that would confront him in efficient discharge of his duties. Acts of oppression and suppression, fear of the rich and the temptations of filthy lucre have been brought into play all over the world to gag the press, not to speak of unfortunate India where even in ordinary circumstances the press has often to face innumerable difficulties in the mere expression of public opinion. All this can be safely attributed to our slavery, political as well as mental. This slavery is the root cause of our helplessness and discomfiture. Is it not then our sacred duty to shake off the shackles eating into the very vitals of our nation? Besides the Government, there are also other forces which are bent upon thwarting the honest working of the press. It is really a herculean task to cleanse the Augean stables and to steer the ship of journalism clear of many dangerous rocks-the iron grips of many potentates, irresistible temptations of mammon and innumerable other evils to which human nature is heir. This is not all. A journalist has to keep his readers abreast of the changing events of the ever- changing world, expose the crooked designs of the authorities and to give vent to public opinion in such a way that its grievances may be redressed, wrongs rectified, rights preserved and democratic principles upheld. In short, all-round duties of a journalist consist in condemning high-handedness, uprooting cruelty, defending the oppressed and downtrodden, putting a stop to injustice, helping to provide food for the hungry and employment for the unemployed, removing social evils, and imparting education to the public for their mental and spiritual development.

"The press has always proved a great blessing to any nation. It has maintained public morale and saved the people from degeneration and extinction in the darkest hour of national history when all other sources failed to guide the country. To quote an instance, the British Press has stood the nation in good stead and has rendered invaluable services at the present critical juncture in saving the country from the darkest clouds. It is no small measure due to the press that today the allies are visualising the immediate prospects of victory.

"The valuable part played by the Indian Press in infusing the spirit of nationalism among the people constitute a glorious landmark in the history of our movement for freedom. Let us cast a glance on the ancient period of Indian history when the people loved to regard their kings as the incarnation of God, and guided by the same principles of Divine Right of Kings, they felt no hesitation in looking upon the British Government as the *'Mai Bap'*; and let us also visualise the present-day India which sees its very salvation in raising the slogan of envisaged above cannot be overemphasized. Despite the political gulf and other differences of opinion, the Indian press has left no stone unturned to uphold those democratic principles for the preservation of which the Allies today claim to be fighting. We wish the Indian press were as free and unfettered as that of independent countries. It would have then made known to the world that it could perform wonders in safeguarding all the more zealously the principles of truth and justice. But to me the freedom of press does not mean the freedom whose fanciful vision is conceived by the fertile brain of Sir Sultan Ahmed, Information Member, the Government of India.

"In Indian States the freedom of press is only nominal which is perhaps the out of our being miserably in a State of double slavery. So far as Jammu and Kashmir State is concerned the freedom of press is a novelty. Though the press is of recent growth here, it is not devoid of absorbing interest. I hope you would permit me to give brief history of the growth of press in the State, and to show how it came into existence. Before 1924, there was neither any newspaper nor was the Government prepared to permit any paper to be started. I fully remember the time when in April 1921, the State Government did not consider it even advisable even to entertain my application for starting a paper in the State. Another application which was made in May 1921, for the same purpose, was, however, entertained but it was ordered thereon that the starting of a newspaper could not be allowed. A third application was made in April 1922, but I was informed in reply that the Maharaja was not inclined to grant the required permission. At last on March 18, 1924, these efforts were crowned with success when the Maharaja-in-Council was graciously pleased to accord permission to a paper being started by me. A sum of Rs. 500.00 was deposited as security with the District Magistrate. Thus on June 24, 1924, came out the Ranbir, the first newspaper of the State. Till first July, 1932, no other paper was allowed to be started. During this period a great awakening and momentous changes were taking place all over the world and the people of the State could not remain unaffected by them. In view of the rapidly changing conditions, the Jammu and Kashmir Government was obliged to relax to some extent the iron grip of its press law. As a result thereof some facilities were for the publication of newspapers. The number of papers and magazines that appeared during the course of these eleven years can be estimated to be in the neighbourhood of 100. Some of them ceased publication because of financial stringencies and other unavoidable difficulties, a few fell victim to the policy of the Government. At present their number is about 50. But this does not and should not by any means connote that the press in Jammu and Kashmir wields power or is in any way the true mouthpiece of the public opinion. The reason for this is not for to seek; a large number of papers for their very existence on the mercy of the Government. The financial condition of most of the papers is usually far from satisfactory. Even from the point of view of standard some of them reveal a deplorable state of affairs. They are tolerated and sometimes helped by the Government merely because their existence instead of being custodian of the rights of masses, is beneficial only to the administration. In order to maintain this state of affairs, the Government has clearly devised a classification of papers which usually compel most of them to curry its favour by hook or by crook. This classification is given three-fold form. To the A-list belong those fortunate papers which are the recipient of precious 'Royal-Robe' in the shape of Government advertisements. The B-list papers are favoured with all sorts of press notes and communiques which they are expected to publish without any remuneration. In the C-list are huddled together those papers which are worst offenders in the eyes of the Government and they are deprived of all the benefits and charities accruing from the publication of official advertisements, notes etc. The most striking feature of this classification is that a paper can be arbitrarily from one list to another at the sweet will of the Government which has a made to rule to revise these lists every six months. The standard of classification which is fixed by the concerned department is merely an eyewash. This classification of papers is strictly an Alladin's Lamp in the hands of the Government by which it can ingeniously make the ordinary papers dance to any tune. This arbitrary classification has not only strengthened the hands of the Government to take full advantage of the financial handicaps of most of the papers but is also contributing to the lowering of the standard of the State press. It is quite evident that this method does not become of a civilizes Government nor it should ever be tolerated by a votary of journalism. The sooner this classification is done away with, the better will be it for the proper cultivation of journalistic standards.

"The State press has yet another grievance to ventilate. It is but rarely that the Government has tried to take the press into its confidence and availed itself of its co-operation in matters of public importance. But for this there would not have existed a wide gulf between the viewpoints of the Public and the Government. The absence of such an important body at a Press Advisory Committee, even at the present critical times through which we are passing, is a conclusive proof of the fact, if proof at all is needed, that the State Government is quite indifferent to the importance and power of the press. In order to ascertain the greatness and power of the press. I would refer here to the valedictory speech recently delivered by His Excellency the Viceroy of India, Lord Lilithgo, in the Central Legislature, in which he rightly recognised the meritorious services of Press of India.

"Besides, the newspapers in the State have to face another calamity these days – the scarcity of newsprint which has endangered their very existence. These are newspapers that have not received at all any quotas or Ration Cards and those who are fortunate in getting them, are experiencing numerous difficulties in procuring the requisite newsprint. It, therefore, behoves the Government to adopt better and more effective measures to discharge its duty in this respect so that paper may enjoy a breathing space in the present suffocating atmosphere.

"I have also to make a few submissions to my brother journalists. Though it is presumptuous on my part to suggest anything to such luminaries as I find sitting before me, yet the responsibilities that you have devolved on me to preside over your deliberations necessitate that I should make bold to say a few words in this connection. Journalism occupies a very high position in society and to maintain its prestige is the sacred duty of every journalist. For the accomplishment of this task no amount of sacrifice is too big. The press is not only free intrinsically, but it has also taken upon itself the responsibility of being the torchbearer of liberty for all the human beings. The press is a mighty force which can be used entirely according to your own selected angle of vision. It is up to you to use it for destructive or constructive purposes. The power of the press, you must know, is neither a gift bestowed on us by any capitalist nor an estate conferred on us by any Government. It is a trust placed in our hands by the people and to use it honestly is our conscientious duty. We should not be led, rather misled, by any communal considerations nor anything else should 'dwarf' us in the efficient discharge of public duties. This power of press should certainly be exercised without any fear, favour or prejudice in uprooting cruelty and injustice and in advocating the cause of the oppressed and down-trodden, the inarticulate labourers and farmers and the dumb-driven indigents. No heed should be paid to any sectional or communal, narrow or personal considerations. We should not be sentimental but realistic and should whole-heartedly follow the dictates of natural laws in this respect.

"At present our country is passing through difficult times. We are surrounded on all sides by clouds of darkness. It is for us to light the torch of guidance to lead the people through the right path to a safe destination. Our masses are steeped in illiteracy and ignorance and hunger stares them in their face. Is it not our bounden duty to ventilate the grievances of the helpless and the oppressed and try our level best to get these redressed? We have also to bring home to the people no form of capitalistic Government is acceptable to us but only a full-fledged responsible Government under the aegis of His Highness the Maharaja which only can act as a panacea for all our ills.

"The world is in the throes of all-embracing total war which is adversely affecting our lives. We shall have to deliver our country from its evil affects. It is high time that we should present a united front to all the enemies of freedom and democracy, but it is only possible when we sink our differences, forget our senseless quarrels, and regard ourselves as the sons of the same soil which should be the touch-stone of our equality and brotherhood. The conviction that a national movement can alone raise us from the depth of humiliation and lead us into the goal of freedom, must be our political creed. Had the Government of India the sense of sobriety and the patience to listen to the voices of the press and sought the co-operation of national leaders, the existing deadlock would have been conspicuous by its absence. We are of firm conviction that if even today this co-operation is sought, the present difficulties would vanish in no time. This would make our country absolutely safe from the onslaught of our enemies and keep high the flag of freedom and democracy similarly the co-operation of the Jammu and Kashmir Government with the national leaders to whom the welfare of our masses is dear to their heart, can guarantee better times for us and can transform our adversity into prosperity. It is just possible that the political jugglers, who in order to amuse themselves or keep the Government in good humour, are misleading the country with their ever-changing somersaults, may prove useful for achieving their private ends, but these tactics are quite untimely which acting like the intoxication of opium will induce a profound slumber on the country from which there will be no hope of its awakening for centuries to come.

"My last but not the least request is that nothing can be accomplished without an organisation and so long as the journalists do not work as an organised body, they can never attain success. We have to reckon with a large number of our enemies and hostile forces and we shall have to be on the quiver to save ourselves from their evil designs. We have got to be fully armed to combat and destroy evil, but this is only possible when we are well organised, know how to make a common stand and consider it to be our duty to sacrifice our individuality for the sake of collective good. It is then and then alone that we can fulfil our mission, glorify our profession and safeguard our rights."

The Conference concluded on August 21, 1943. The Amrit Bazar Patrika reported among other things "About 8,000 people attended it. Besides the journalists, prominent citizens, municipal commissioners, Assembly members, lawyers, professors, doctors, business magnets and public leaders were present. Among those on the dais included Rai Bahadur Himmat Singh, Revenue Minister, Sheikh Abdullah, President National Conference, and Pandit Jia Lal Kilam, President Bar Association. About 60 journalists from the State and half a dozen from the Punjab participated in the deliberations".

# CHAPTER 11

# Prime Minister's First Press Conference

For the first time in the history of journalism in Jammu and Kashmir, the representatives of the Press were invited to meet the Prime Minister of the State in his office at a press conference in Jammu on February 13, 1944. The room which is now occupied by the Full Bench of the State High Court in the old secretariat premises, was packed to capacity.

Sir B.N. Rau took over as Prime Minister from Sir K.N. Haksar on February 9, 1944. On February 12, 1944, the new Prime Minister expressed his desire to meet the press and exchange views with them. A meeting of the All Jammu and Kashmir Editors' Conference was held in the office of the Ranbir same day. Shrimati Shakuntla Seth, Chief Editor the Usha, presided. It was attended, among others, by Pandit Prem Nath Kannah, Mr. R.K. Kak, representative of the United Press of India, Pandit Vishwa Nath Kerni, Pandit Shambhu Nath Koul, Mr. Balraj Puri, Choudhry Mohd. Din, Editor the Al-Insan, Mr. Yakin Ali Maskin, Editor the Kisan, Mr. Ghulam Mohi-ud-Din of the Khidamat, Bakshi Bodh Raj, Editor the Kashmir Mail, Mr. Om Prakash Saraf, Editor the Rattan, Raja Mohan Akbar Khan, Editor the Sach, Mirpur and Pandit Bhag Mal, Editor the Bharati. The question was as to how best to probe the mind of the Prime Minister and how best to let him know the views of the State journalists regarding conduct of the affairs of the State, came in for thorough consideration at the meeting.

At the Press Conference next day, the Prime Minister accompanied by the Chief Secretary Lala Haveli ram and the State Publicity Officer Pandit Shankar Lal Koul faced more than thirty newsmen. The session lasted for 100 minutes. Sir B.N. Rau addressing the newsmen said that he had thought it proper to meet the journalists collectively instead of individually. He stated that he had come to try to make Jammu and Kasmir a model State for which he needed co-operation of others, particularly the press which he considered to be a mighty power for achieving the good provided the pressmen realised their responsibilities. Asserting that he welcomed all healthy criticism. He stated that he had been told that most newspapers indulged in attacks against the State officers. He, therefore, suggested that before publishing such criticism, the editors should also personally approach the Publicity Officer for proper action in the matter. In the absence of any action on the part of Government, the matter should be brought to his notice at the next press conference; thus alone the press could render the real public service, the Prime Minister added.

There was a volley of questions put by the newsmen who had been rather taken aback by the Prime Minister's suggestion. As it was the first Press Conference addressed by Prime Minister, the Ranbir gave it full publicity and even published names of those journalists who had put questions to him. For this the Ranbir had to apologize for the departure from the long-held convention not to disclose the names of the questioning newsmen. It will interest many to know how the pressmen in the State had foiled the attempt by the Prime Minister at his very first Press Conference to curb their legitimate activity which his suggestion really implied. Here are reproduced some of the important questions a d answers high=lighting inter alia few of the burning problems of the day.

Mulk Raj Saraf (Ranbir): Journalists should not be bowed down that before publication they should first refer complaints to the Publicity Officer. Once the editor is convinced that any allegation are bone fide, he should as a matter of necessity publish them. It is our right to do so. To assert our right, we are prepared to take our risk. Whatever we have to say to the Government, we say it through our papers. If the allegation turns out to be incorrect, the officers concerned can get them contradicted or any other step may be taken in the matter.

Prime Minister: Mine was a mere suggestion. I did not prescribe any prescribe any law.

R.K. Kak (U.P.I.): A Srinagar newspaper published certain allegations against an officer. Its editor was arrested under the Defence Rules. He was handcuffed and paraded through main thoroughfare. Could not the proper action be taken according to the law? The editor could be sued for defamation. If you desire co-operation from the Press, you should also show due respect to the pressman.

Prime Minister: The matter is sub-judice.

Mulk Raj Saraf: Our complaint is against the procedure adopted by the Government; why the editor was handcuffed?

Prime Minister: I have noted it.

Girdhari Lal Anand (Firdous): At present whatever is published is in the press against the Government officials, it is sent in the form of newspaper cuttings to the officials concerned for the explanation. Do you envisage to stop this procedure?

Prime Minister: To forewarn is to forearm. Prior publication of allegations causes hinderance in the course of inquiry.

Raja Mohd. Akbar Khan (Sach): If we have got a grievance against an official, are we to send from there (Mirpur) a diary to the Publicity Officer.

Prime Minister: You can wite a letter to him.

Raja Mohd. Akbar Khan: Would not our position be reduced that of a C.I.D. man?

No reply.

Ram Saran Das Malhotra (Zindagi): It is no occasion and to use to interfere in the freedom of press in the presence of laws at present in force in the State.

Prime Minister: My view is that by adopting the course I have suggested, the Government will be greatly helped. If it is very tedious and impracticable, I will not press it.

Girdhari Lal Anand: My personal experience is that the 'White List' of newspapers whereby newspapers have been divided by the Government into A, B and C classes, entirely cuts across the freedom of the press. It is unheard of anywhere else in the world. It should be scrapped.

Prime Minister: I have noted it.

Kaviraj Vaishno Gupt (Desh Sewak): Whenever we ask the authorities to give reasons for removing the name of a paper from ;White List' we are told the matter is confidential.

Mulk Raj Saraf: An editor is also a man liable to commit mistakes. Let the editor against whom the Government intends to take any action, be first given an opportunity to explain what he has got to say in the matter. If his reply is found unsatisfactory, the matter should then be referred to a Press Advisory Board whose decision should be final.

No reply.

Ramsaran Das Malhotra: In my opinion all Government advertisements to newspapers should be stopped forthwith. This will enable the newspapers to tread the right path. It will also finish the bogus newspapers and their guides. No distinction is observed here between a good paper and a bad paper. A newspaper may have a circulation of only ten or it may have a circulation of ten thousand, both are treated alike by the Government. Of what avail are such papers to the Government. If you stop the Government advertisements, the bad newspapers would die automatically and good newspapers would survive and thrive.

No reply.

Kaviraj Vaishno Gupt: It has been published in some newspapers that before you came here, you met Mr. Jinnah. Prime Minister: I have met Mr. Jinnah several times.

Kaviraj Vaishno Gupt: After your appointment as Prime Minister of Jammu and Kashmir, have you discussed State politics with Mr. Jinnah?

Prime Minister: No.

Chaudhari Mohd. Shafie (Sudarshan): The real demand of the people of the State is the establishment of a responsible Government under the aegis of Maharaja Bahadur. What help you intend to render to the people in this connection?

Prime Minister: It is too big a question.

Om Prakash Saraf: The question is also being put to the biggest authority in the State.

No reply.

Kumari Shanta (Bharti): Would you also consider the plight of women in the State?

Prime Minister: I have noted it.

Kumari Shakuntala (Usha): Would you also meet a women's delegation?

Prime Minister: yes. I have noted it.

Dinu Bhai Pant (Gulab): Would the Government notices, notifications and orders be published in Hindi also?

No reply.

Abdul Majid Qureshi (Pasban): You have stated that justice will be done to all. There are 78% Muslims in the State. But only one day after you took over as the Prime Minister, the Revenue Minister nominated 4 Muslims, 4 Hindus and 2 Sikhs as Naib *Tehsildars*.

N.D. Nargis (Chand): The Muslim League has given a prominent place in a map of proposed Pakistan. What do you think about it?

Prime Minister (after a little pause); I do not want to say anything.

K.H. Khurshid who later became the so-called President of "Azad Kashmir" Government (Javed): Despite their population being 78% of the State, the Muslims are not getting a fair deal. How do you intend to remove their grievances?

Prime Minister: Whatever would be done for the betterment of the State, the biggest majority inhibiting the State would proportionately be the biggest beneficiary.

Prime Minister Rau like his immediate predecessors did not remain in the saddle of premiership for long and during his short tenure of office, Jammu and Kashmir could make little headway much less become a model State which he had desired it to be. Reputedly a great constitutional Pundit, he was much occupied, even during the period he was Prime Minister in the State, with great changes that were in the process of being introduced in British India in those days. Once as a Chairman of the Hindu Law Committee, he was absent from the State for full 100 days. During this period, Nawab Jafar Ali Khan, Development Minister, officiated as the Prime Minister. Mr. Rau's long absence from the State gave rise to persistent rumours that he was disinclined to come back. It was rather ridiculous to find that after Sir Gopalswamy Aiyengar every Prime Minister, however otherwise eminently known or qualified, was finding it hard to stick to his job. The State, it was openly said, was proving to be a graveyard for many a reputation. It was in this context that a patriotic urge compelled me to personally approach Maharaja Hari Singh to set the matters right so far as the quick succession of one Prime Minister after the other was concerned. I fully knew that the Maharaja could not be willing at all to grant responsible Government to the people of the State. The appointment of two popular Ministers chosen by the Praja Sabha as a sort of diarchy was considered by the Maharaja more than sufficient in the circumstances prevailing them. The Ranbir was, no doubt, a staunch supporter of responsible government under the aegis of the Maharaja as was being strongly advocated by the National Conference. But the deadlock had to be got over. I felt there was need to do away with the 'import' of outside Prime Ministers who continued to come and go. Accordingly on January 18, 1945, which was the *Basant* day, I sent the following telegram to the Maharaja who was then staying in Bombay:

"I as loyal subject and son of the soil claiming to know some public mind beseech Your Highness with folded hands to declare yourself Prime Minister as well in case Sir B.N. Rau does not come back as reported in Press. Today is Basant: end of one season. Let there also be an end of repeated appointments of Prime Ministers from outside. Your Highness becoming Prime Minister for which precedents exist, can bring many boons to suffering people and vouch safe speedy reforms in administration leading to responsible Government under Your Highness' aegis."

The Maharaja did not accept my suggestion which proved to be a voice in the wilderness. He, however, appointed on June 29, 1945, a son of the soil, Pandit Ram Chandra Kak, Minister-in-waiting to His Highness, to succeed Sir Rau as the Prime Minister.

# CHAPTER 12

## Kakistocracy

What followed the installation Mr. R.C. Kak as the Prime Minister is strictly speaking beyond the scope of this book. Suffice it to say that the Kak regime came to be known as Kakistocracy. The Ranbir also fell victim to it.

Mr. R.C. Kak had risen to the high position sheerly by dint of hard work and intelligent discharge of his duties. He was the first Government employee to occupy this position. His relations with the Editor of the Ranbir had been very friendly. In his appointment, the Ranbir naturally saw a dream being fulfilled in as much as a talented son of the soil had become the head of the administration. Even Sheikh Abdullah hailed the appointment of whom he described as the first Kashmiri-speaking Prime Minister of the State.

But as an irony of the fate, the cordial relations between Mr. Kak and the Ranbir were sooner than later, manifestly under heavy pressure resulting from their different approaches the most delicate situation, the State was confronted with on the eve of the partition.

In May 1946, Sheikh Abdullah had launched his famous 'Quit Kashmir' movement. This he did without consultation of the Congress High Command and in a manner that smacked of regionalism. For instance, in one of his public speeches, he attacked the Maharaja for pursuing a policy which allowed grant of *jagirs* to some Jammu people in the Kashmir Valley without granting any *jagir* to even a single Kashmiri in the Jammu region. Such criticism of a Maharaja who was in no way alien, considering the State as a whole, was not approved by the Ranbir as well as many top congress leaders excluding, of course, Pandit Nehru.

Meanwhile Sheikh Abdullah had also been declared as the President of the India States' Peoples' Conference in place of Pandit Nehru who was going to be elected the President of Indian National Congress. On May 20, 1946, Sheikh Abdullah was arrested. Pandit Nehru wanted to defend him in the Court but was stopped by the District Magistrate, Srinagar, Pandit Maharaj Kishan

Dhar, at the Kohala bridge. In his characteristic style, Pandit Nehru broke through the police cordon and reached Domel where he was detained in the Government Rest House. The Ranbir recorded its strong protest against the official handling of the situation at a moment when the country was engaged in a very serious dialogue with the British Government regarding the transfer of power to the Indian people. Pandit Nehru, however, left the State following a call from the Congress High Command.

The writing on the wall was clear to the Ranbir. India was going to be not only freed but also partitioned as a result of growing tension between the Congress and the Muslim League. Fortunately for Kashmir, her popular movement as spearheaded by Sheikh Abdullah, had no love lost with the Muslim League and its leader Mr. Mohammad Ali Jinnah whose bid to personally woo the Kashmir leaders had failed earlier. But the tensions between the Maharaja and the Kashmiri leader made the prospect of Kashmir, making its contribution towards the consolidation of the nationalist forces in the country extremely difficult. The Ranbir could not but strongly stress the need for immediate release of Sheikh Abdullah who was undergoing 3 years' imprisonment in Bhaderwah jail following the Quit Kashmir movement which the Sheikh had later declared to be 'not against the person of the Ruler but against the autocratic regime'. Simultaneously the Ranbir demanded the accession of the State with the Indian Union. But Prime Minister Kak had developed his own outlook and approach. With a personal friendship spread over almost 25 years he seemed to expect from the Editor of the Ranbir an active support for his viewpoint. On the other hand, I was honour bound to strenuously work in the direction which I, in all sincerity, felt to be right. Soon arose the important question of the Indian States joining India's Constituent Assembly set up to frame the Constitution of free India. Several princely States chose to send their representatives to the Consembly. The Jammu and Kashmir Government, however, hesitated to take up any timely action in the matter. The Ranbir bitterly criticised the vacillating policy of the Government. In this connection the Ranbir which had become *daily* since December 1, 1946, in its editorial of March 15, 1947, quoted a statement made by the then Prime Minister Gopalswamy Aiyengar on the floor of Praja Sabha on April 4, 1942, when pressed by the members for information as to what the attitude of the Maharaja and the State Government was in relation to Sir Stanford Crisp's Mission that had arrived in Delhi from London in connection with constitutional changes in India. He had said:

"Kashmir's attitude will be one of welcoming the formation only of a single Union for the whole of India (cheer) and the State will do its utmost to co-operate with the works of framing a constitution for it so that when the constitution is made, it may find itself able to accede to it. The Jammu and Kashmir State and the State's people will, I have no doubt, not look with favour or any tendency towards the formation of a multiple Union in the country and in consequent disruption of which is now and what should in future continue to be a United India.

The Ranbir in its issue of April 6, 1942, had described the speech as welcome addition of a magnificent chapter in the modern history of India.

The Ranbir decried in forceful language such attempts as seemed afoot on the eve of national independence to keep Jammu and Kashmir aloof from India and characterised this move as a big conspiracy against the State. Such criticism greatly upset Mr. Kak. Once he Head of the Information Department told me with eyes almost wet that the Prime Minister had chided him more than once for his failure to win my favour. "Starve Mr. Saraf" into submission, Mr. Kak wrote ultimately on one of the files of the Information Department. Secret instructions had gone round not to send any advertisement to the Ranbir, not even to subscribe the Rattan – the children's journal published by me, for any educational information.

This was indeed little price to pay for the historical role which the Ranbir was destined to play in a most crucial hour of the nation's destiny. The Ranbir continued to emphasize its twin demand for the release of Sheikh Abdullah and the accession of the State to India. Every morning the demand was prominently front-paged in a panel. Mr. Kak had, however, found powerful allies in Jammu where the prominent Hindu leaders had been given the impression that the Maharaja after the lapse of the British Paramountcy would do well to steer clear of India and Pakistan and even expand the kingdom later on. It may appear incredible now but it is a part of history that while repeatedly voicing a course of action which it considered to be absolutely in the interest of every section of population in the State, the Ranbir had to face considerable resistance from the Jammu Hindu leaders. Once the copies of the Ranbir were made a bonfire of by some angry Hindu young men in public thoroughfare of Pacca Danga of Jammu town.

The matters with the Ranbir came to head when Acharya J.B. Kriplani, the then President of the Indian Nation Congress, visited Jammu on May 24, 1947, on a good-will mission. It was generally believed that his visit to the State was to study the situation on the spot and impress upon Maharaja the desirability of releasing National Conference leaders including Sheikh Abdullah.

Acharya Kriplani stayed in State Guest House. I went to meet him. As I was talking with the distinguished leader, Mr. Kk suddenly entered the room and asked the Acharya to enquire from me about the present attitude of the Sheikh. Though somewhat taken a back, I told the President of the Congress, it would be possible for me to know the mind of Sheikh Abdullah if Mr. Kak permitted me to interview him in the Bhaderwah jail. The matter ended there but Mr. Kak was apparently a bit nervous over his failure to secure a diplomatic hit, though a good diplomat he undoubtedly was.

Only four weeks after the incident, I was served with a notice by the District Magistrate, Jammu on June 25, 1947, reading:

"I, Chet Ram Chopra, District Magistrate, Jammu hereby direct for the purpose of securing public safety and maintenance of public order and in exercise of the powers conferred upon me by rule 35 of the Jammu and Kashmir Defence Rules as continued in force by Section 2 of the Emergency Provisions (Continuance Ordinance No. 111 of 2003) read with Notification No. B-437/45 P.B. forming annexure to Council Order No. 750-C of 1945 dated 6th August, 1945, that you shall not till further orders make use of the printing press named Prem Printing Press for the printing of any newspaper from the date of this order.

Given under my hand and seal of the Court this day the 9th of Har, 2004."

As if this alone was not sufficient to crush me, another order, reproduced below, was simultaneously served on me. It read:

"I, Chet Ram Chopra, District Magistrate, Jammu, hereby direct for the purpose of securing public safety and maintenance of public order and in exercise of the powers conferred upon me by rule 35 of the Jammu and Kashmir Defence Rules as continued in force by Section 2 of the Emergency Provisions (Continuance Ordinance No. III of 2003) read with Notification No. B-437/45 P.B. forming annexure to Council Order No. 750-C of 1945 dated 6th August 1945, that you will not till further orders make use of the printing press named Prem Printing Press for the printing of any newspaper from the date of this order.

Given under my hand and seal of the Court this day the 9th of Har, 2004."

There was obviously no previous warning, nor any security demand. No grounds whatever for the action set forth in the arbitrary orders. Scores of people were working in the offices of the Ranbir and its Printing Press. With one stroke of pen all of them were thrown out of job foe no fault of theirs. What more than this could there be indeed to "starve Mr. Saraf?"

On the day the orders were given, I was in Srinagar. The orders in Jammu were served on the Assistant Editor of the Ranbir – Om Prakash Saraf – at 9 in the night. Earlier in the morning the Additional District Magistrate had summoned him in his office and told him that as it would take some time to go through certain formalities in preparing the orders, the Ranbir should not be published on that day. To this the Assistant Editor had spiritedly replied that it was not possible to postpone the publication of the paper on verbal orders. Perhaps the authorities were yet awaiting full instructions from the Government in Srinagar.

On being informed on the telephone of the whole affair, I immediately issued the following press statement from Srinagar:

"In view of the efforts that were being made in diverse ways to put pressure on the Ranbir during the past some months and the way the Ranbir was resisting those tactics, the prohibitory orders, regarding the Ranbir and its Printing Press were not unexpected. Such orders cannot subdue my spirit, nor undermine my determination. The efforts for the accession of the Jammu and Kashmir State to India as well as release of Sheikh Abdullah and other National leaders which were being strenuously made by the Ranbir in the interest of real and everlasting benefit of the State and its Ruler, would continue unabated."

The national press as well as the entire local press stood aghast. Even the pro-Pakistan newspapers like the Inqilab, Lahore, took the Government to task for its 'inhuman step'.

The conscience of the government was perhaps also pricked. A spokesman of the Government suggested to me to express regrets to the Government and get the prohibitory orders rescinded. Another VIP approached me to ask for an undertaking for good behaviour in the future and everything will be all right. I also received hints to put in representation asking in plain words for the resuscitation of both the Ranbir and the Printing Press and this surely be done. I listened to all these things and kept mum as I had no doubt in my mind that the Maharaja himself, if he did not get rid of his lot of advisers, was bound to come to grief. While a good deal of harm had already been done, Mahatma Gandhi paid a visit to the Maharaja in Srinagar in July, 1947. This paved the way for Mr. Kak's exit who was soon to lose his job and much more. On August 10, Mr. Kak was succeeded by Major General Thakur Janak Singh-retired Revenue Minister. Most people heaved a sigh of relief. A deliverance day celebrated by the National Conference.

On August 26, 1947, I received the following orders from the District Magistrate, Jammu:

"I hereby withdraw my order dated the 9th Har, 2004 prohibiting you from printing and publishing the daily Ranbir."

A similar order removing the ban on my Printing Press was also issued.

The stand of the Ranbir was vindicated but alas, the State had lost a golden opportunity to accede to the Indian Union in time.

# CHAPTER 13

# Accession to India

The Ranbir stood gagged at that fateful hour when India was happily freed but tragically partitioned. The Jammu and Kashmir Government on its part had failed to take a timely decision about its future affiliation. The controversy whether Mr. Kak himself favoured an independent State of Jammu and Kashmir or he simply carried the behests of the Ruler in supressing the pro-India forces of the day, may, perhaps, be never resolved. But it is clear that the powers-that-be did favour a non-aligned status at a time when the futility of such an unrealistic policy could hardly be more obvious. Confronted with distressing circumstances emerging from its own prolonged apathy towards fast moving political scene, the State Government was left with no other choice but to enter into stand-still agreement with both India and Pakistan.

A Government Press Note issued on August 12, 1947, read:

"Prime Minister of Jammu and Kashmir has wired to the States' Relations' Departments of India and Pakistan to say that the Jammu and Kashmir Government would welcome stand-still agreements with them on all matters on which there exist at present moment with the outgoing British India Government.' It has been suggested that existing arrangements should continue pending settlement of details and formal execution of fresh agreements."

Another press note issued on the same day said:

"His Highness The Maharaja Bahadur has been pleased to order that the 15th, the 16th and the 17th August, 1947 be observed public holidays throughout the State and the towns of Jammu, Srinagar, Gilgit and Leh illuminated on the 15th to celebrate the establishment of Dominions of the Union of India and Pakistan and retrocession of Paramountcy."

The Ranbir re-emerged on September 10, 1947, when the all-important question of the State's relationship with India was still pending solution. The Amrit Bazar Patrika had reported an interview with the Maharaja asserting that he could sign a decree for the union of the State with Pakistan with his life blood only. Nevertheless, he carried on parleys with the Simla Hills chiefs and other princes presumably to carve out an extended independent kingdom for himself. He was also believed to be constantly in contact with Delhi, London and Karachi to keep himself adequately informed about their reactions to his move. Meanwhile Pakistan had accepted the offer by Jammu and Kashmir of the standstill agreement but India true to its declared policy of thrashing out matters with the popular leaders of the various States rather than their hereditary rulers, made explicit its reluctance to enter into any such agreement. The Ranbir vigorously resumed its campaign for the release of Sheikh Abdullah and the State's succession to India. Paradoxically speaking, nothing strengthened the hands of the pro-India forces in the State more than the crude tactics adopted by the unscrupulous rulers of newly born State of Pakistan. The standstill agreement with them soon proved to be an illusory nature. Quite against the provisions of the standstill agreement, Pakistan withheld all essential supplies like salt, sugar, patrol and cloth to the State. Pakistan's real aim in doing so was to starve the population and thus coerce the State to join it. Pakistan also restored to various other inhuman methods to achieve its objective. It excited locals in Poonch to rebel against the authority of the Maharaja a thinking. The popular leaders of the State including even those Hindus who earlier appeared to favour independence now cried for early release of Sheikh Abdullah and accession to India. Due to prevailing uncertainty, general situation in the State was fast deteriorating.

The Maharaja could resist no more. Sheikh Abdullah who had earlier been brought from Bhaderwah to Badami Bagh, Srinagar was ordered to be released on September 29, 1947. Gradually all other imprisoned leaders were also set free. Sheikh Abdullah in his first public utterance after his release declared at Hazuri Bagh, Srinagar, on October 1, 1947, that "till the last drop of my blood, I will not believe in two-nation theory or formation of States on basis of religion." He also stated at the same meeting that first of all he wanted to have full responsible Government in the State which could then choose between India and Pakistan. He, however, more than once showed his inclination towards what he called India of Gandhi and Nehru.

In the meantime ended the interregnum of Prime Minister Major General Thakur Janak Singh who was permitted by the Maharaja on October 13, 1947, "to relinquish the post of Prime Minister at his own request for reasons of health". Mr. Justice Mehar Chand Mahajan took over as Prime Minister the same day. The same evening he held a press conference at which he declared that he wanted to make Kashmir Switzerland of Asia. Mr. Mahajan stated:

"I am assuming the charge of the office of Prime Minister at a moment when the State is on the chessboard of power politics. I am here in a spirit of loyal service to the ruler and his people. I am optimistic enough to say that in the dominions of His Highness, the East and west Punjab will once again meet as friends and I come with an open mind and have no rigid political creed or theories. I am satisfied that the constructive work for one's country irrespective of ideologies is what is needed the most at the present moment. I do believe that the Government of His highness must be so run that it takes its decisions with the co-operation and consent of the people's representatives and is ultimately responsible not only to His Highness but also to his people."

The great merit of Mr. Mahajan lay in the fact that besides an eminent Judge of men and matters, and endowed with a congenial temper and a progressive mind, he enjoyed full confidence of both the Maharaja and the Government of India. Personally speaking, my relations with Mr. Mahajan were as they continue to be, most cordial. I had succeeded him as the President of the All-India Mahajan Conference held in Shakargarh in 1931. In 1942 when he again presided at the annual deliberations of the All-India Mahajan Conference held in Jammu, I was the Chairman of the Reception Committee Incidentally, it may be recalled that Sheikh Abdullah sent me from Srinagar his warmest congratulations on adopting a resolution at the Jammu session of the Mahajan Conference in connection with the liquidation of rural indebtedness.

Before actually assuming charge of the office of Prime Minister, Mr. Mahajan had a few meetings with Sheikh Abdullah in Srinagar. These talks generally cantered round the question as to how far the National Conference was prepared to cooperate in the task of governance of the State. The day Mr. Mahajan took over, Sheikh Abdullah left for New Delhi for talks with Pandit Nehru and also to take formal charge as President of All-India States' Peoples' Conference. Probably at the instance of the Sheikh, one of his trusted colleagues, Pandit Jia Lal Kilam resumed the thread of talks with Mr. Mahajan. Pandit Kilam took me along with him to Mr. Mahajan. I never enquired from late Pandit Kilam whether he was taking me with him to meet the prime Minister of his own accord or he had been advised by Sheikh Abdullah to do so. We both had a few meetings with Mr. Mahajan on October 15 and 16, 1947. Our discussions were confined to two points; first, participation of National

Conference in the State Council of Ministers and, secondly, the portfolios to be allotted to the National Conference Ministers.

Prime Minister Mahajan insisted that Sheikh Abdullah and Mirza Moh'd Afzal Beg should themselves join the State Cabinet. Pandit Kilam opined that in case the National Conference accepted office as a result of mutual understanding, as nominees should necessarily get Home and Finance portfolios. Mr. Mahajan invited me to tea alone in the evening of October 16, 1947. We had a long talk discussing various facets of the question before us. The next morning I met Mr. Kilam. As a result of my conversation with him, Pandit Kilam on the following morning addressed a note to the Prime Minister in which he said:

"I had a talk with Mr. Saraf and gathered an impression that my submission require some further elucidation. May I, therefore, request you to kindly make it possible to permit me to meet you at any time convenient to your good self today."

The word today as underlined by Mr. Kilam significantly marked the urgency of the occasion. But things were moving too fast mainly due to the growing intransigence and daily increasing aggressive activities of Pakistan on the border areas of the State. Mr. Mahajan had to immediately undertake a tour of those areas, first in the valley then in Jammu. So he hurriedly wrote back in his own hand on Mr. Kilam's note and handed over to me: "I think we will meet next week. I am going out of Srinagar."

On October 23, 1947, the armed tribesmen from Pakistan crossed into Kashmir through Muzaffarabad. They were soon on their way to Srinagar. At Garhi, the Chief of Dogra Army, Brigadier Rajindra Singh had to lay down his life to stop advance of the marauders. On the night of October 24, The Dussehra Day, Srinagar City was plunged into darkness as the power-house in Mahoora had been badly damaged by the raiders. The same day Mr. Ram Lal Batra who was the Deputy Prime Minister, left Srinagar for New Delhi with a formal letter of succession of the State to India., from Maharaja Hari Singh, along with a personal letter to Pandit Jawahar Lal Nehru, Prime Minister of India, and another to Sardar Patel, the Union Home Minister asking for military aid to save the State from Pakistan's approved aggression. Sheikh Abdullah also flew to Delhi on October 15, 1947.

Meanwhile disquieting news continued to pour in Srinagar from Poonch and Baramulla sides. Advance of the raiders to the City of Srinagar had to be stopped at any cost. At this critical junction, Mr. V.P. Menon, Secretary of the Union Minister of States, flew from Delhi to Srinagar on October 25. It was decided that the Maharaja should go to Jammu to be easily available, if situation so demanded for personal negotiations with India and that Mr. Mahajan should immediately accompany Mr. Menon to Delhi by air.

How the Government of India took decision to give military aid to the Maharaja to drive out the armed tribesmen has been vividly described by Mr. Mahajan in his book "Looking Back":

"Next morning (October 26) Mr. V.P. Menon and I flew to Delhi. We arrived at Safdarjung airport at 8 A.M. where a car was waiting. I immediately drove to the Prime Minister's House on York Road. The Prime Minister and Sardar Patel both were there and were apprised of the situation that had arisen. In view of the advance of the raiders towards the towns of Baramulla and Srinagar, I requested immediate military aid on any terms. I said somewhat emphatically that the town of Srinagar must be saved at any cost from loot and destruction. During the talk, the Prime Minister said that even if the town was taken by the tribesmen, India was strong enough to re-take it. Its recapture, however, could not have undone the damage that would have resulted. I, therefore, firmly but respectfully insisted on the acceptance of my request for immediate military aid. The Prime Minister observed that it was not easy on the spur of the moment to send troops as such an operation required considerable preparation and arrangement, and troops could not be moved without due deliberation merely on my demand. I was, however, adamant in my submission; the Prime Minister who was also sticking to his own view. As a last resort I said, "Give us the military force we need. Take the accession and give whatever power you desire to the popular party. The army must fly to save Srinagar this evening or else I will go to Lahore and negotiate terms with Mr. Jinnah."

"When I told the Prime Minister of India that I had orders to go to Pakistan in case immediate military aid was not given, he naturally became upset and in angry tone said, 'Mahajan go away,' I got up and was about to leave the room when Sardar Patel detained me by saying in my ear, "O course, Mahajan, you are not going to Pakistan." Just then, a piece of paper was passed over to the Prime Minister. H read it and in a loud voice said, "Sheikh Sahib also says the same thing." It appeared that Sheikh Abdullah had been listening to all this talk while sitting in one of the bedrooms adjoining the drawing room where we were. He now strengthened my hands by telling the Prime Minister that military help must be sent immediately. This came as a timely help for the success of my mission to New Delhi. The Prime Minister's attitude changed on reading this slip. After a few minutes talk, he told me to go and have some rest at Sardar Baldev Singh's house. He was calling a meeting of the Defence Council at 10 A.M. to discuss the matter and promised to convey its decision to me through my host, Sardar Baldev Singh (the Defence Minister) before lunch.

"I left the Prime Minister's house and went to the house of Sardar Baldev Singh. After a shave and a bath I retired for some needed rest. During the previous three days I had neither time for sleep nor rest. At 12.45 p.m. Sardar Baldev Singh came and told me that a decision had been taken to send two companies of Indian troops to Srinagar. All the planes in India had been requisitioned for the purpose. He also wanted me to give the commander of this force as much information as I could about the situation in the State. Luckily, I had brought with me a plan which showed where the clash between the raiders and the State forces had occurred, the deployment of the raiders and distribution of the State forces.

"The Cabinet meeting in the evening affirmed the decision of the Defence Council to give military aid to the Maharaja dive out the tribesmen. Around dinner time, the Prime Minister sent a message to me that with Mr. V.P. Menon I should fly to Jammu to inform the Maharaja of this decision and also to get his signature on certain supplementary documents about the succession. I frankly informed him that I was not prepared to go to Jammu till I got news from my aerodrome officer at Srinagar that the Indian forces had landed there. Panditji did not insist and said, "you can fly to Jammu next morning."

"In the early hours of the morning of 27th, I could hear the noise of the planes flying over Sardar Baldev Singh's house and carrying the military personnel to Srinagar. At about 9 A.M. I got a message from the aerodrome officer of Srinagar that troops had landed there and had gone into action. On receipt of this message, I flew to Jammu with Mr. V.P. Menon. As we landed in Jammu, the Brigadier of the State forces met me. He felt considerably relieved that the troops on landing in Srinagar had gone into battle with tribesmen. Mr. Menon and myself met His High at the palace. This had created some confidence in his mind. After some discussion, formal documents were signed which Mr. Menon took back to Delhi."

Sheikh Abdulla also returned to Srinagar after military operations by the Indian army had started.

On November 2, 1947, the Sheikh was duly sworn in as the Head of the Emergency Administration. He took all the prominent members of the National Conference in the Administration. To maintain public relations closely between the State Government and Government of India, Bakshi Tek Chand ex-Chief Justic Punjab High Court, was summoned as the representative of Jammu and Kashmir State in New Delhi and Kanwar Daleep Singh India's agent in Jammu and Kashmir State.

The Ranbir, of course, hailed the accession of Jammu and Kashmir to India as well as the association of Sheikh Abdulla and his top colleagues with the Government although the delay in effecting a change of such far-reaching significance had left much to be desired. The State was fully experiencing the horrors of a full-scale war.

# CHAPTER 14

# Silver Jubilee

On June 24, 1949, the Ranbir completed its twenty-fifth year when India was no longer in bondage. The national leaders though deprived of the guidance of Mahama Gandhi who was shot dead by a fanatic Hindu on January 30, 1948, were striving hard to frame a constitution of free India. Jammu and Kashmir had acceded to India but an uneasy Indo-Pak ceasefire prevailed which still continues. The popular Government in the State had been installed but Maharaja Hari Singh after handing over the power to his talented son Yuvraj (now Maharaja) Karan Singh had left for Bombay for good. The revolutionary measures being introduced by the National Conference Government had enraged the feudal, reactionary and communal elements in the State. Also at the helm of affairs had emerged several adventurists and unscrupulous people devoid of competence and capacity as fit instruments of a social change. The occasion hardly provided a happy spectacle to celebrate the Silver Jubilee of the Ranbir with much festivity. It, however, issued in 118-page special issue inter alia containing many messages of good wishes from all over the country. Some of these may be read with interest here indicating what a great institution the Rambir had been able to develop into during 25 years of its life:

His Excellency Shri Rajagopalachari, Governor General of India: "The biggest single influence that today moulds the progress and character of a people is the newspaper. May the Ranbir continue its good work for many more years to come."

*With the staff of RANBIR and its printing press on the occasion of*
*Silver Jubilee of the paper (June 1949)*

Dr. B. Pattabhi Sitaramayya, President, Indian National Congress: "That your paper should have struggled and survived a quarter of century with all its vicissitudes, is not a small matter. I congratulate you on your successful career and that it will lead to a still greater success."

Sheikh Moh'd Abdulla, Prime Minister, Jammu and Kashmir State: I feel happy to send my felicitations to Lala Mulk Raj Saraf, veteran journalist and the founder-editor of the first newspaper published in the State. The Ranbir has been leader of thought in many matters and I testify that many dreams it has dreamt have come true."

Shri N. Gopalaswamy Aiyengar, Minister of Transport and Railways, Government of India: "I remember reading the Ranbir regularly when I was in Kashmir (As Prime Minister). Its outlook was progressive throughout and, while it gave expression to fairly strong criticism, it was not afraid of supporting those in authority when it felt that they were in right."

Shri B. N. Rau, India's permanent Representative with the United Nations, Lake Success U.S.A.: "Much has happened in Jammu and Kashmir since I left for the State but I hope that the Ranbir is still flourishing and hat it will continue to flourish in the years to come."

Shri Devdas Gandhi, President All India Newspapers' Editors' Conference: "I congratulate the Ranbir, the well-known nationalist daily, published in Kashmir on its having completed 25 years of useful service."

Dr, Siddheshwar Varma, Editor, the Great English Indian Dictionary and ex-president the Linguistic Society of India: "When generations hence the history of Jammu and Kashmir will be written, the Ranbir will certainly be characterized as one of the makers of Jammu and Kashmir. It has been said that men make history, but ideas make men. One of the fountain heads of history making ideas has been stimulating journal Ranbir."

Pandit Sham Lal Saraf, Health and Local Self Government Minister Jammu and Kashmir: "To have run the paper successfully for twenty five long years and to have consistently held and espoused views of progressive character was not task of a man of ordinary calibre."

Sardar Budh Singh, Minister for Information, Broadcasting, Law and Constitution, Jammu and Kashmir: "It was no ordinary task of its Editor, Lala Mulk Raj Saraf, that the Ranbir in spite of great hardships and opposition, voiced forth the feelings of the oppressed and depressed people of the State."

Colonel Pir Mohd. Khan, Education Minister, Jammu and Kashmir: "The Ranbir from its very inception has been advocating the popular cause of liberty, peace and progress and has fought for its success. It has always been its unfailing endeavour to strengthen the bonds of friendship between Kashmir and India so that through harmonious understanding and unity of efforts they may serve the common good of mankind."

Shri Rana Jung Bahadur Singh, Editor the National Call and the Nav Bharat and an ex-Editor of the Times of India: "Mr. Saraf is one of those veteran journalists who have placed their talents as an offering at the altar of the goddess of liberty. The Ranbir fought many a battle on behalf of democracy in Jammu and Kashmir and today after its twenty-five years of heroic efforts the joy of witnessing the speedy crystallization of its dreams. If its silver jubilee is really silver, let its Golden Jubilee be truly golden."

Shri Tushar Kant Ghosh, Editor The Amrit Bazar Patrika: "May the Ranbir continue to help in the noble mission of creation of an ideal secular State in beautiful Kashmir within the Indian Union."

Shri Janaki Nath Wazir, Chief Justice of Jammu and Kashmir High Court of Judicature: The Ranbir has had a brilliant and glorious career. It has grown from strength to strength during these twenty five years of life and looks forward to an even more successful career in the future. It has been expressing the mind of the public without fear or favour and has always avoided writing on communal subjects which might offend feelings of one community or the other. The paper has strived hard to bring about communal harmony between different sects of people in this country."

Shri Dwarka Nath Kachru, Private Secretary to the Prime Minister Jawahar Lal Nehru: "Twenty-five years ago when the Ranbir was first started, there was hardly any paper worth the name in any of the Indian States. The Ranbir had a humble beginning but as time went on, it made progress and assumed responsible position in the public life of the State."

Mr. G.A. Ashai, a prominent Kashmiri intellectual: "I have keenly watched the progress of this paper and I know how, amidst the difficulties and adverse conditions through which our State has had to pass, the Ranbir continued unstinted to give support to the progressive voice of the people."

Pandit Radha Krishan Kak, journalist, Srinagar: "The story of the foundation and progress of the Ranbir is in itself a glorious chapter in the history of journalism in Jammu and Kashmir. The steadfastness, uprightness and fearlessness with which Lala Mulk Raj Saraf served the cause of the country through the Ranbir have set up a very high standard of journalism in the State."

Pandit Lok Nath Sharma, ex-Advocate General, Jammu and Kashmir: "The policy of the Ranbir in upholding the rights of the people even in advance circumstances gives credit to Mr. Saraf of which any front-rank journalist may feel proud."

Major General Bishan Das, retired Prime Minister of Jammu and Kashmir: "I will remember the time when Lala Milk Raj Saraf was making efforts to bring about, he first newspaper of the State. It was no easy task. Shri Saraf, however, by dint of his determination and ability made impossible the possible. He has set an excellent record worthy of emulation by his selfless service to the country in general and the people of the State in particular. I used to read the Ranbir regularly so long as my eyesight worked. Still I am getting the paper read out to me regularly.

Justice Kishan Lal Kichlu, a former President of the State Legislative Assembly: "The liberal, non-communal and national outlook of the Ranbir has earned for it great popularity. Mr. Mulk Raj Saraf should indeed feel happy that the several constitutional and other reforms as advocated by the Ranbir has now assumed a practical shape."

Saradar Dewan Singh Maftoon, Editor the Ryasat, Delhi: "It is no easy task to bring out a successful newspaper from any princely State but Mulk Raj Saraf has creditably led the way to journalism in the Indian States."

Pandit Baldev Prasad Sharma, Journalist: "I feel proud that I learned A.B.C. of journalism at the feet of Lala Mulk Raj Saraf. I was a student at Shri Pratap High school, Srinagar, when in 1927, I began to send news stories for publication in the Ranbir. I was particularly instructed by Lala ji to keep a copy of all that I sent to the Ranbir and then compare it with what appeared in the paper. I was at first disappointed because I found my despatches so much 'mutilated' but later on I realised its value and gained tremendously thereby. During 25 years' existence of the Ranbir. The conditions in Jammu and Kashmir have considerably changed. In this the Ranbir and its editor have played a conspicuous part and they can rightly feel proud of their achievements. Journalism in the State has indeed greatly advanced under the guidance of the Ranbir."

Dr. S.S. Nishat, Kashmir Trade Agent in Bombay: "I began my career with the Ranbir. The Ranbir has brought forth in lime-light many big and small personalities, I myself, being the smallest among them. I met Sheikh Abdulla and other State leaders for the first time in the office of the Ranbir. The foundation of the Jammu National Conference was also laid in this office of the Ranbir. Due to his farsightedness and uprightness Lala Mulk Raj Saraf has had deep vision of the future."

Shri Prem Nath Pardesi, noted story-writer: "As a school boy I used to read the Ranbir with much interest. Then I began to write for it. When for the first time, my name appeared in the paper, I felt overjoyed as if I had become a great man and that I had the power to practically change the whole world. I composed some poems which Shri Mulk Raj Saraf published in his paper after suitable corrections. This greatly encouraged me. In fact I owe my literary career to the Ranbir."

Pandit Ganga Nath Sharma, a former Joint Editor of the Ranbir: "It would be no exaggeration to say that the seed of democracy which we see thriving in the State today was implanted and nourished with full caress and determination by the Ranbir in the course of last 25 years in face of great hardships and adverse conditions. The dream of yesterday as dreamt by the Ranbir, has become a reality today. What aspect of life is there for the improvement and progress of which the Ranbir has not made the right use of its forceful pen and reasoning? For rendering this selfless service, Lala Mulk Raj Saraf took up the journalistic enterprise at a time when there appeared hardly any chance for the success. There were the callousness of the officialdom, the opposition of the reactionaries and the vested interests, the lack of interest in newspaper reading by the people, the non-existence of any source of collecting and sending news, the shortage of writers and correspondents. These were enough to unnerve the determination of any experienced editor of a newspaper, but Lala Mulk Raj Saraf bravely faced all this and came out with flying colours in the field of journalism."

# CHAPTER 15

# Parting of Ways

Sheikh Abdullah had not an easy start. In the very nature of the circumstances in which the power was transferred to him, the fissures were bound to occur sooner than later, on the one hand, between him and those in authority who had never seen eye to eye with him and, on the other hand, within his own camp between him and those like him who had neither the experience nor the patience to deal with an admittedly nerve-breaking attention that had arisen as a result of the wanton Pakistani aggression.

The Sheikh was appointed by the Maharaja as the Head of the Emergency Administration on November 2, 1947. This brought into being, as the Ranbir put it, two rival administrations in the State- Sheikh Abdulla enjoying popular support with best wishes of Nehru Government in Delhi and Mr. Mehr Chand Mahajan who continued to be the Prime Minister 'with their respective sphere of powers and positions totally vague, undefined and unclarified.' The Sheikh was sometimes called the Head of the Emergency Administration and sometimes the Chief Minister, Similarly, Mr. Mahajan was described as the Prime Minister as well as the Dewan.

Once I told Mr. Mahajan that the appointment of the Sheikh, his own fate as the Prime Minister had been sealed. He brushed aside my idea little realising that I knew the Sheikh better than he did. The Sheikh began to do whatever he wanted in the name of emergency not unoften without even informing the Maharaja, much less the Prime Minister. The confusion continued till the Sheikh whose star was in ascendency, was formally installed as the Prime Minister on March 17, 1948, when the Maharaja in deference to the wishes of the Government of India announced the establishment of full-fledged responsible Government in the State presumably with the immediate view to strengthening the hands of India in the Security Council. Mr. Mahajan left the State after terminating the agreement of service which allowed him handsome compensation for the unexpired period of his five years' term but which he did not claim. A little longer the Maharaja himself had to leave the State after Yuvraj (now Maharaja) Karan Singh in his late teens, was made the regent.

So far so good. Sheikh Abdullah as the most popular leader of the State especially at that critical juncture of the history while stoutly defending the cherished ideals of secular democracy and radical social change, indeed deserved and amply received the whole-hearted support of all well-wishers of the country. For the Ranbir, it was truly the realisation of long dreamt dream in the shape of the popular government in the State. It threw open its columns to publicity aiming at the stabilization of the regime which was being constantly attacked not only by the standard-bearers of democracy across the border but also by the reactionary elements within the State itself. The Ranbir did much more. Its Assistant Editor, Om Prakash Saraf, offered his wholetime services and worked in an honorary capacity as the Emergency Publicity Officer. And how hard he worked would be evident from what the Deputy Head of the Emergency Administration, Bakshi Ghulam Mohammad, noted on January 2, 1948:

> "I am glad to bring on record my deep appreciation of the voluntary and honorary services of Mr. O.P. Saraf as Emergency Publicity Officer in absence of any official machinery pertaining to propaganda and publicity work in Jammu. His ability in immediately organising the office and efficiently carrying out the multifarious responsibilities entrusted to him in very abnormal times has greatly impressed me."

The Ranbir later assailed the agitation launched by the Praja Parishad (now Jan Sangh) for merger of the State with the Union as ill-conceived and strongly opposed it. It is interesting to recall that Praja Parishad's first charter of demands *inter alia* urged the imposition of a ban on the publication of the Ranbir. In fact, the Praja Parishad leadership consisted of the same old people who had earlier never approved of the policy of the Ranbir favouring the State's immediate accession with India. Since, however, it had become a *fait accompli*, with their privileges fast disappearing, they raised the demand for a complete merger with the Indian Union, motivated by a desire to wash off their old sin as also to embarrass the Kashmir leaders without sharing their responsibility in any way to strengthen the willing association of the Muslims in the valley with the rest of the country.

The Pakistan press in those days when all means of communication were completely cut off between the two parts of the State that had come to be divided by a cease-fire line under United Nation's observance, would occasionally exploit the good name of the Ranbir presumably to hoodwink its innumerable admirers there. (Many years later in May, 1964, my eldest son,

Om happened to visit Rawalpindi. Choudhry Ghulam Abbas, the top leader of Pak-occupied Kashmir sorrowfully told him that he had to leave his hometown Jammu because there were not "a few more like you at Jammu.") For instance, the Dawn of Karachi published in its issue of May 11, 1949, a news-item circulated by the Associated Press of Pakistan from Abbottabad attributing to the Ranbir an article from the pen of 'a writer, a professor in local college' saying "Kashmiris whether Hindus or Muslims are deadly against the Abdullah cabinet and solidly behind the Muslim Conference's demand for accession of the State to Pakistan". I was in New Delhi where this canard came to my notice on May 12, 1949. I immediately issued a press statement from Delhi saying:

"This is a complete fabrication and a white lie characteristic of the Dawn like Pakistani Press. It is most shocking, particularly because the news item is stated to have emanated from a premier news agency of Pakistan. The Ranbir can never give place in its columns to such baseless, false and irresponsible statement. The Ranbir has consistently championed the cause of nationalism from its very inception and as such has always given its full and willing cooperation to the Administration headed by Sheikh Abdullah."

When the Ranbir celebrated its Silver Jubilee on June 24, 1949, Sheikh Abdullah was good enough to acknowledge its services in a long message. But this was actually a feeble cover for the strains and stresses that had begun to raise their ugly head in the relationship between the Head of the Government and the Editor of the premier newspaper of the State after about twenty years of mutual goodwill. I am still appreciative of his many qualities of head and heart. But as a dispassionate newspaperman, I had to judge the Sheikh in his new role as an administrator. His weakness lay in the fact that he would take national view of things only when it fitted in with his egoistic inclinations. Though he did introduce quite a few reforms of far-reaching significance, their working left much to be desired with the result that the Ranbir had to be critical at times. This extremely annoyed him.

At one time I told Sheikh Abdullah in his office in Srinagar "Shiekh Sahib, you are always rightly claiming that you have rid the people of Maharaja Hari Singh. But would you believe that you have imposed on them more than one Maharaja". Enraged over this he burst out:

"I am already receiving reports about your changed attitude towards us. I would not any longer listen to you much less act upon your advice. If you persist in your present behaviour, I am afraid, I shall have to send you to the Central Jail (pointing his finger towards the Hari Parbat Fort)".

When I wrote to Om in Jammu as to what had happened between the Prime Minister and myself, pat came the reply from him:

"You might have told the Sheikh that you have not been enjoying such a life as if put in jail, you would have to suffer much".

The Sheikh had permitted himself to be surrounded by a set of sycophants who were always busy in poisoning his ears to grind their own axe. They were afraid of the Ranbir and would, therefore, leave no stone unturned to wean the Sheikh away from the Ranbir. Once I had an occasion to talk over things in Jammu and Kashmir with a high officer of the Indian Foreign Service in Delhi. He soon reported this conversation to one of the advisers of the Sheikh, who on my return to Jammu, told me:

"You take advantage of your being the premier journalist in the State and malign the men in power here."

I said in reply: "I am not habituated like you to say one thing to one man and another thing to another man or say something by mouth and write something else on paper. If I have told my Delhi friend something our Prime Minister, I must have said the same thing in the face of the Prime Minister himself or published the same in my paper. Have you not observed similar criticism in my paper? My views are not hidden from anybody. As for my being a premier journalist in the State, you cannot undo history however you may desire to do it."

To stifle the voice of the Ranbir, Sheikh Abdullah's advisers began to adopt tactic which were more responsible than even those adopted by an autocratic regime in the past. They misuse secret funds and financed publication of newspapers whose copies would be distributed among the people free of charge. The Government advertisements were withheld. Even some private advertisers were persuaded to terminate connections with the Ranbir. It would not be even subscribed in any school or other official or semi-official agency. Those who privately subscribed to the Ranbir were regarded as political untouchables. Om, who had by then become active in the political field, was ousted from the National Conference. And, attempts were made to purchase the die-hard reactionaries including the communalist who had every reason to be angry with the progressive policies pursued by the Ranbir. The Ranbir, thus, found itself by an intriguing combination of circumstances, between the devil and the deep sea. Of course, the past of the Ranbir could not be obliterated nor the spirit of the Ranbir which manifested itself for such a long time in bringing about much needed reforms in various spheres of public life, could bend. The Ranbir, I strongly felt, had done its duty by the people. Better to stop it now and here and keep its glorious past alive rather than compromise. I had to spend many a sleepless night to ponder over the closure of the Ranbir just as I had to work day and night to bring it into being.

On May 18, 1950, the Ranbir chose to disappear. On that day the announcement of the closure reproduced below took its readers by surprise: "With heavy heart it is announced that due to various reasons which need not be mentioned at present, further publication of the Ranbir cannot be continued. I am, therefore, compelled to close the paper indefinitely."

It was indeed an irony of fate that the Ranbir – the physical part of it – fell victim to a popular regime for whose establishment it had worked so hard and long and that and that during the time of a leader who, though only a college student when the Ranbir came into being, had grown in the years to come, with a good deal of mutual understanding with the Ranbir. It was no consolation a few years later to find the 'victor' himself falling victim to his thoughtlessness.

# CHAPTER 16

# As a Newsman

With the disappearance of the Ranbir, I ceased to be an editor but not a journalist. Henceforward my role was confined to being a newsman – a reporter on behalf of several prominent newspapers in the country. I had my early training as a reporter with the 'Bande Matram' in 1920. The reminiscences of the proceedings at the Town Hall, Lahore. Of the Hunter Commission which the British Government had set up to enquire into Jallianwala Bagh massacre still thrill my heart. I vividly remember how Shri Jagat Narayan, an eminent Judge of the Allahabad High Court, who was a member of the Commission, would pounce upon General Dyer to know about details of the tragedy.

As the Editor of the Ranbir, I had literally to create reporters all over the State. All this helped me in course of time to possess a proper understanding of the rights and responsibilities of a newsman. In the discharge of my obligations as a newsman in the strategic State, I often encountered many a difficulty at the hands of those who had little respect for the sacredness of the facts.

It may be in the fitness of the things to mention here that the leading news concerns in the country invariably took the initiative in asking for my services as their correspondent in the State. Mr. P. Dutt, Editor-in-Chief, the Free Press of India, (later United Press of India) wrote to me on September 23, 1928: "On the suggestion of one of my friends, I am glad to write to you requesting you to work for us as our correspondent". I accepted the job. Three months later, the Editor in his letter of December 24, 1928 said: "You have laid us under a deep debt of gratitude by supplying us very many interesting news items. I am happy to inform you that your dispatches are very much appreciated here."

Mr. A.S. Iyengar, Editor, the Associated Press of India, New Delhi, in his letter of December 30, 1930, wrote: "We hereby request you to send us all available news in Kashmir State for the use of the Associated Press." Mr. G.F. Crawley, news-editor of the Statesman, in his letter on January 29, 1931, said: "We shall be glad if you will act as our correspondent for the Jammu and Kashmir State, sending stories of first-class interest." On March 8, 1932, the

Statesman Editor wrote to me : "I understand that Col. Colvin, the new Prime Minister of Kashmir State, desires to see you for a friendly discussion of the question of news. In a recent letter of yours, you said that you found difficulty in getting news and I think your talk with Col. Colvin, the difficulty will be settled," Later on, I met Col. Colvin and made certain suggestions regarding release of official stories which he was good enough to appreciate and accept.

Pandit Amolak Ram on the eve of his retirement as Editor the Tribune wrote: "During my stewardship of the Tribune you have always extended to me hearty cooperation and help in improving the news side of the paper. I feel but for your cooperation the position of the Paper would not have been as unassailable as it is today. I am writing this letter to express my grateful thanks to you for what you have done for the Tribune."

I have been representing some leading national dailies now for nearly four decades. I do not know of any occasion when my news story could be authoritatively contradicted. Of course, the authorities did occasionally use their power arbitrarily to punish me for disclosure of newsworthy facts unpalatable to them. I have always held the view that a news story should contain nothing but fair and impartial presentation of facts without any attempt to minimise or exaggerate them. A correspondent should scrupulously avoid a personal bias or local prejudice or laying the colours too thick on one or the other aspect of an incident.

While there can be no end to the risks-financial, mental and even physical, that a conscientious newsman will have to continue to face at the hands of totalitarian bureaucrats, unscrupulous politicians and profit-making capitalists, it will be interesting to recall some of the battles that I have had to wage while seeking to function as a newsman, in addition to the few experiences recorded earlier.

## The Internment

Towards the end of July 1937, a Division Bench of the Jammu and Kashmir High Court consisting of Chief Justice Sheikh Abdul Qayoom and Justice Janaki Nth Wazir (now Chief Justice), reduced the sentence of the accused in a cow-slaughter case from 7 years' rigorous imprisonment to that of one year. It was held that the offence was not committed to wound anybody's religious feelings or susceptibilities but done secretly at night. The Hindus and Sikhs who had already been viewing with concern the Muslim agitation regarding the protection afforded under the law to the cow in the State, got alarmed and held protest meetings. Jammu City observed complete hartal for 35 days. There were processions and hartals in several other towns. There were also several clashes between the police and the demonstrators, hundreds of whom including women were injured. Numerous people were taken into custody. I was duty-bound to collect relevant news on the spot. As a matter of routine, I kept notes of happenings with me. The authorities resolved to prevent the truth from going out. On August 23, 1937, I was manhandled, arrested and removed by the police to the city lock-up where I was kept for several hours. It was only after the arrival there of District Magistrate, Col. Baldev Singh Pathania, that I was let off. Next day, however, I was externed from the city under an order reading: "Whereas it has been made to appear to me by credible information that you, Lala Mulk Raj Saraf, are fanning the present Hindu agitation, I, Col. Baldev Singh Pathania, District Magistrate, Jammu Province, Jammu, being thus satisfied that your activities are causing breach of the peace and disturbances of public tranquillity and spreading hatred against the Government, hereby give directions by virtue of the powers vested in me under section 108-A Cr. P.V. clauses b, c and d that you shall remove yourself from Jammu town and shall remain in town of Samba for a period of six months and shall not deliver any speech in any public meeting within the aforesaid period or participate in any activities. Given under my hand and the seal of the Court this 10th of Bhadun 1994."

It may be mentioned here that there was never an occasion for me to deliver any speech or participate in any other activity except to work as a newsman.

In fact my presence in Jammu was regarded so dangerous that I was not later permitted even to pass through the town to attend the contempt proceedings pending against me before the Full Bench of the Jammu and Kashmir High Court. I had to undertake journey from Samba to Srinagar via Rawalpindi.

The Jammu Journalists' Association placed on record their deep sense of resentment at the 'barbarous maltreatment meted out to a press representative'. Prominent leaders like Sheikh Abdullah, Lala Hans Raj Vakil and Pandit Jia Lal Kilam expressed their shock and sorrow. An old brother journalist Pandit Vishwa Nath Kerni announced that he would not in protest publish his paper till my return to Jammu. The Tribune on September 3, 1937, editorially wrote: "In all civilized countries press representatives enjoy immunity from harassment and undue restriction. In fact, they are provided with facilities by the authorities for performing for performing their duties satisfactorily. We are, therefore, surprised to learn that the Kashmir Government has removed Lala Mulk Raj Saraf from Jammu where he has been functioning as a correspondent of several responsible newspapers, including Anglo-Indian journals and interned him in a village. The publication of reports regarding lathi-charges and arrests at Jammu may be distasteful to the officials but that is no reason why a press representative should be deprived of his liberty. Either it should be proved that Mr. Saraf has been guilty of an offence against the State or he should be set at liberty."

The Quami-Dard, a leading English weekly at Srinagar edited by Shri D.N. Bazaz, wrote: "Mr. Mulk Raj Saraf is a pioneer journalist of the State who enjoys an inter-provincial fame. There has not been a single official or non-official of Kashmir so far who has not paid a glowing tribute to his high sense of responsibility and patriotism. Col. Colvin who was the Prime Minister of Jammu and Kashmir only a few months ago, is reported to have said about Mr. Saraf that he conducted his paper like a true responsible journalist and always steered clear of communalism. But it was after all left for the present Government to see in Mr. Saraf a "dangerous" person whose presence in Jammu had placed the peace of the country in jeopardy. Does it go to the credit of the Government to intern such a responsible journalist and public man on no evidence whatsoever? We may be accused of using strong language but as a well-wisher of the Government, nothing would pain us more than finding that the Government because of a hasty action has lost its reputation for justice and fair play. We make a strong appeal to Prime Minister Gopalaswami Ayyangar that he may personally go through the papers pertaining to Mr. Saraf's internment case. Mr. Ayyangar has a reputation of being an enlightened administrator. It is not too much to hope that he will undo a wrong that has been gratuitously done to a pioneer journalist and a publicman of our State."

Ultimately on the basis of certain assurances contained in a proclamation of Maharaja Hari Singh regarding cow-protection, the agitation which the High Court judgement had touched off, was called off. Consequently under orders of the Maharaja all the arrested people were released and all prosecutions pending in the Courts were withdrawn. Bonds taken for keeping the peace or being of good behaviour were also cancelled. My externment came to an end on September 23, 1937. The contempt of Court proceedings against me also dropped.

## The 'Roti' Agitation

In 1943, Jammu city underwent a great suffering in what is known as the 'Roti' agitation resulting from soaring prices and scarcity of food grains. The Ranbir fully brought the acuteness of the situation to the notice of the authorities but in vain. The common hardship united all sections of the local population as rarely before. There were mass meetings and processions protesting against official apathy which was indeed callous. On September 24, 1943, thousands of town men including many women took out a procession in defiance of the order prohibiting assembly of five or more than five persons. When the processionists reached the city chowk, they were first lathi charged and then fired at. This resulted in instantaneous death of seven persons and injuries to many others two of whom also died later. The city was immediately placed under curfew and the Army was called to control the situation. The army units paraded the lanes in the evening bugling that the martial law had been enforced and anyone daring to come out of his residence would be shot dead. The authorities later, however, refused that any martial law had been imposed.

The State Assembly had commenced its autumn session in Srinagar as scheduled on September 25, 1943, but it was prorogued by the Maharaja in view of the seriousness of the situation in Jammu. The Prime Minister, Colonel Sir Kailash Narayan Haksar, and the Revenue Minister, Shri Himmat Singh Maheshwari, were deputed to make a sifting enquiry on the spot. The Maharaja also donated Rs. 50,000 from his private purse for the relief of distress caused by the scarcity of food supply in Jammu. Maharani Tara Devi and Yuvraj Karan Singh, too, contributed Rs. 5,000 each for the purpose. Shops for the sale of foodgrains at cheap rates were opened at once.

The Ranbir had to rise to the occasion. It vividly reported how the authorities had first miserably failed in assessing hardships of the public, and then perpetrated atrocities on them. The reports published in the Ranbir were being widely quoted by the Lahore press to condemn the State Government. The Prime Minister soon after his arrival from Srinagar called me and Om Saraf who as the Assistant Editor of the Ranbir had in a signed leading article given his eyewitness account of the situation captioned "the barbarous madness of the inefficient and oppressive authorities." The Revenue Minister was also there. They accused us of having actually started and inflamed the agitation. A long argument followed. And in the end the Prime Minister was so much moved that he delivered us a cheque for Rs. 5,000/- which he desired me to distribute to the firing-sufferers. I later appointed a citizens' committee and got the money disbursed.

Meanwhile, the people persisted in their demand which the Ranbir wholeheartedly supported, that an impartial enquiry be immediately held to find out the truth. Accordingly the Maharaja appointed a 3-member inquiry committee presided over by Sir Govind Madgaonkar, a retired Judge of the Bombay High Court and including Justice P.K. Sen and a member of His Highness's Board of Judicial Advisers and Justice Quazi Masud Hussan, a Judge of Jammu and Kashmir High Court. The town resumed normal work after 9-day hartal.

But my job was not yet done. When the inquiry committee commenced its proceedings in Jammu on October 20, the Public Defence Committee headed by Lala Roop Chand Nanda, a brilliant member of the local bar, who was later assisted by the well-known national leader, Dr. Saif-ud-Din Kitchlu Barrister-in-Law, thought of producing me as their first witness before the public body. This meant more of tension between the Ranbir and the authorities. Nevertheless, I had no choice but to uphold the right cause. When in course of my deposition I was asked by Chairman Madgaonkar as to what the Government officers stationed in Jammu were doing all the time to ease the situation. I politely replied, 'they were asleep'. I well remember that my innocent yet well-pointed remark created a great stir in the Committee Hall and the Chairman had to admonish the audience to observe strict silence in the Court. For more than a day, I was in the witness-box under a heavy fire of cross-examination by the Advocate General, my esteemed friend, Pandit Lok Nath Sharma.

The report of the enquiry committee was never made public. But this resulted in the dismissal and demotion of several officers which was a clear indication that their case had failed, thus amply vindicating my role as a newsman.

## Sheikh Abdulla's Arbitrariness

The readers should be now well aware of the important milestones in the labyrinth of journalism in the State. In the early 1920's the August Ruler would not be even prepared to entertain a request for bringing out a newspaper. In early 1930's factual report of the local demonstration against Gandhi Ji's arrest would earn the total ban on the publication of the only newspaper in the State simply because the Ruler wanted to make his position clear in the eyes of the British Government. In 1937, during the time of Prime Minister N. Gopalaswamy Ayyangar, a reporter could be locked up and then externed from the Capital without even being told what story circulated by him was considered objectionable. In 1943, Sir Kailash Narayan Haksar, the then Prime Minister would not shirk in seeking to make a journalist a scapegoat in order to protect his officers responsible for shooting dead nine citizens. In 1945, Shri B.N. Rau another Prime Minister appeared on the scene with the bold statement that he wanted to make Jammu and Kashmir State a model State but he had felt little hesitation in suggesting to the local newsmen at their first ever conference with a Prime Minister, to send to the Government all papers received by them against any officers before publishing them. The newsmen, of course, did rise to a man to defend their right to publish all reports at their own risk. It was left to Mr. R.C. Kak, the first Kashmiri-speaking Prime Minister, to ban the premier newspaper in his territory for making a vigorous plea for the accession of the State to Indian Union. It, however, fell to the lot of Sheikh Abdullah – the first popular Prime Minister of the State, to create conditions for the disappearance in 1950 of the first and foremost newspaper of Jammu and Kashmir which had fought longer than he for the cause of the people.

As to how arbitrarily the Sheikh and his officers behaved in respect of the press, would be clear, apart from the foregoing account, from a few typical incidents. On August 25, 1949, the Governor and District Magistrate, Jammu, Lala Brinda Ban 2 ordered me not to publish or send any news regarding Praja Parishad agitation unless it was verified by himself. The Ranbir while opposing the agitation had published that the police had made indiscriminate arrests taking into custody even those who in no way were connected with the agitation. The order of the District Magistrate stated: "The news published in the Ranbir is not only unauthenticated but to say the least irresponsible also and that cannot be expected from a newspaper of the standing of the Ranbir." Assuming that to be true, what sin the outside newspapers, whom I represented and whom the order had sought to deprive of my service, had committed? The order on the face of it made a fantastic reading and was, of course, soon withdrawn.

After the Jammu and Kashmir Constituent Assembly had been set up, Sheikh Abdullah sought an assurance from the Government of India that the ratification by the Consembly of the State's accession to India would be accepted as final. This Pandit Jawahar Lal Nehru did not concede although he would not prevent the Consembly from expressing its view in the matter. Undoubtedly an awkward position confronted the Sheikh: his verdict as the leader of the Consembly was not quite binding on the country for which he stood while the country he opposed was sparing no propaganda to destroy his image as a popular Kashmiri hero. In the meantime, the Sheikh had also actually become somewhat unpopular for his inability to give to the people a clean, efficient and sympathetic administration. In that delicate situation he chose to regain his popularity with unsophisticated people by appearing to be a little neutral between India and Pakistan. In April 1952, he delivered his well-known controversial speech in Ranbir Singh Pura border town indicating a clear rethinking in his part vis-à-vis relationship between Srinagar and Delhi.

Honour bound I reported it to my papers. So did several others including my sons, Om and Suraj. Besides strong public reaction, Government of India was also shocked and probably pulled up the Sheikh who then decided to make newsmen the scapegoat. Within a few days he had an opportunity while inaugurating a canal park in Jammu, to take to task the newsmen for what he described as misrepresenting him. But what clarification he actually made only confirmed his Ranbir Singh Pura speech. The talented P.T.I. representative, Mr. Rajagopalan, rightly reported that what the Sheikh had earlier stated at Ranbir Singh Pura was considered to be factually correct by himself. I had also reported to my papers more or less in the same strain. This further enraged both the Sheikh and his critics for their own reasons with the result that the political situation began to worsen rather speedily.

Upon this, Mr. Rajagopalan was got transferred from the State which made him rather happy. Three of us were served with notices warning us that we could be deprived of our privileges as newsmen. As a matter of fact it had been and continues to be all risk to be good reporter in this State. In reply I submitted that I had merely done my duty and I intended to maintain my privileges only by reporting what I thought to be right. My sons also replied in the same vein.

Following the Ranbir Singh Pura speech, came what was called the Delhi Agreement between the State and the Union Government. But it was clear that the Sheikh still had his reservations. The monarchical system was abolished as were the big landed estates. The last of the Dogra rulers

– Yuvraj Karan Singh – became the first elected Head of the State called Sadar-i-Riyasat. But effective steps were not being taken to establish constitutional relationship between the State and the Union as envisaged in the Delhi Agreement. Meanwhile the Praja Parishad started a mass agitation which was seized upon by the Sheikh to project his ideas about the future affiliation of the valley. In April 1953, while performing the opening ceremony of a tube-well near the Jammu Tawi bridge, he stated he would frankly tell Jammu people: "If you cannot live with us, you are free to go your own way, we will go our own. Good-bye."

Yet, to prevent the people outside the State from coming to know the actual state of his mind, a novel technique was evolved. The write-ups were prepared in advance of delivery of his speeches would be circulated to the newsmen who would be asked to confine their reporting to these official versions which were far from factual. I manually resisted all such attempts. Soon the Sheikh was to fall out with far more powerful personalities on the national scene, leaving him little time to clear his accounts with 'smaller fries'.

## Clash with Bakshi

Sheikh Abdullah went off the scene as the Prime Minister on August 9, 1953. Notwithstanding the present widespread sympathy for the man for his past role and prolonged suffering, it may be conceded that administrative standards had gone down considerably during his tenure. Bakshi Ghulam Mohammad who succeeded him, was a far more shrewd and practical man. With such able associates as Dr Karan Singh and Mr G.M. Sadiq by his side together with liberal central aid, the Bakshi soon consolidated his position. He began with very cordial relations with the press as with many others.

It was during his time that I got an opportunity to go on my first ever foreign tour as the sole delegate from Jammu and Kashmir to the First World Congress of Journalists at Helsinki, Finland, in June 1956. My brief impressions of this travel as also the welcome address presented to me on my return home in August 1956, are given in Appendices I and II. Needless to add this 'token of love and respect' is my most cherished possession coming as it does from my associates in the profession.

*A general view of the First World Journalists Meet at Villa Otaniemi Helsinki (Finland) Une 10, 1956; 259 journalists from 44 different countries of the world attended the conference. The members of the Indian Delegation are seen in the front row. The Author with Gandhi cap on, is third from right.*

*With the President of the International Organisation of Journalists, Jean-Maurice Hermann of France (holding each other's arms), at Villa Otaniemi, Helsinki (June 11, 1956)*

The things, however, began to deteriorate after some time. The Bakshi's dynamism was somewhat tempered with disregard for scruples. The power went to his head. His lust for authority appeared limitless. He came to have faith in his world being law and everyman carrying a price. He naturally lost all confidence in his colleagues whom he considered unfit in his scheme of affairs. This caused a split between him and Mr. G.M. Sadiq soon after the general elections in 1957. This was the crucial period for a conscientious journalist.

After parting company with the Bakshi, Mr. Sadiq set up the Democratic National Conference as the State's pro-India opposition party with a considerable following throughout Jammu and Kashmir. This unnerved the Bakshi as he saw in it the prospect of his possible replacement. Where there could be little objectionable in the Bakshi and Mr Sadiq opposing each other, the former was keen to ensure that the views of Mr Sadiq should not be published in the national press. He actually won over a few journalists but found a difficult man in me. Having failed to persuade me to follow his wishes, the Bakshi thought of contacting the newspapermen whom I represented in the State. All his efforts, however, ended in fiasco as my long association with the national press which I had served so passionately with a sense of full responsibility, proved too much for his resourceful machinations.

The Bakshi literally shuddered to think of getting divorced from the political power. In January 1958, Sheikh Abdullah was released from long detention. This was most unpalatable to him but he could hardly murmur in view of the known policy of the Government of India. Yet, he was so afraid of the Sheikh's coming closer to Delhi that at a press conference in answer to a certain query from me, he as if awakened from a dreamland thrice stated that "Sheikh can never come to power." I had to rather strongly tell him that I never asked if the Sheikh could. The Bakshi soon put the Sheikh again in the jail in April 1958 after taking advantage of the Sheikh's own reluctance to visit Delhi.

Once the State's Inspector General of Police, Mr D.W. Mehra, told me in confidence that he had been asked by Prime Minister Bakshi to haul me up under the Public Security Act, if I did not contradict my story regarding reported occupation by the Chinese of some salt lakes in Ladakh. The Bakshi's game appeared to be that as my story involved the Defence Ministry, I could perhaps be browbeaten. Meanwhile, however, my story had been discussed in the Parliament and the Prime Minister Nehru himself, had made a statement which more or less confirmed my report. I told Mr Mehra that he was free to plan his own strategy to satisfy his angry boss. Thereupon the Inspector General of Police wrote to me a letter asking me to "intimate the source of my information so that proper action may be taken against the person who has been the cause of dissemination of such false and alarming news." As he failed to get any response from me, he got the case registered with the local police. I and my son Suraj, who was representing the Times of India, were summoned to the City Police Station where some silly questions were put to us which we replied suitably. Nothing was heard of the case afterwards. On being informed by me of the episode a prominent editor wrote to me "never mind, you are in a good company."

Why did Bakshi resign under the Kamraj Plan in 1963? Much has been said and written on this subject. The ample answer to it is that he tendered his resignation as he never expected it to be accepted. And it is now on record that as soon as its acceptance was announced, he stage-managed protests to force Mr Nehru to reconsider his decision. I was in Srinagar on the morning following the night when his offer to resign had been accepted. He had arrived from Delhi and was being taken out in a procession by his admirers. I could read from his face the sorrowful sleepless night after getting 'Kamrajed". The Bakshi rightly realised that I could not be party to his heartfelt desire for the comeback. Once during those fateful days he invited local newsmen to a dinner, I was not. There was, therefore, no occasion for me to visit him. The next morning, however, an old brother journalist revealed it to me that the Bakshi in the presence of pressmen had summoned his gate-keeper and instructed him that I had not been invited to the dinner and if I still happened to enter his residence, I should be prevented. Such was his deeply felt longing to supress a dissenting voice. I, on my part, informed my papers and told them that I would not be meeting the Bakshi on any occasion unless and until he made amends. Soon he sent me his apologies – how *bona fide*, I would not say.

## Sadiq's Liberalisation

Bakshi Ghulam Mohammad was succeeded by his nominee Khwaja Shamsuddin on October 12, 1963. Prime Minister Shamsuddin's tenure of office, though eventful, was shortlived. First, because he did not enjoy the confidence of Mr G.M. Sadiq whom Delhi expected to succeed the Bakshi who himself had assured Mr Nehru that he would ensure Mr Sadiq's election as the new leader of the legislative wing of the ruling party. Secondly, because the Bakshi soon got disgusted with Khwaja Shamsuddin who had begun showing signs of independent judgement without, of course, enjoying the support of the party which remained a convenient tool in the hands of the Bakshi.

Prime Minister Shamsuddin was soon to meet his Waterloo when the National Conference party itself and its Government too, proved unequal to the unprecedented situation resulting from the theft of the Prophet Mohammad's sacred hair from the Hazaratbal shrine, near Srinagar, in December 1963. There was a mass upsurge which literally humbled the pride of almost every ruling man except shrewd Mr Sadiq who rode on the popular wave and whom Bakshi, ultimately, in the presence of then Union Minister without portfolio Shri Lal Bahadur Shastri, accepted as the new Prime Minister. Mr. Sadiq was elected the new leader of the State Legislature on February 27, 1964, and was sworn in as the Prime Minister the next day.

Prime Minister Sadiq began with the much-needed promise of introducing what he described in the Press Conference on March 1, 1964, as a policy of liberalization and democratisation. Speaking on behalf of the newsmen, I assured the new Prime Minister of the full support and cooperation of the Press in the State in his efforts to ensure social justice and equity for the common man.

It will be perhaps yet too early to pronounce a judgement on Mr. Sadiq's role as Head of the Government, For, the plain fact is that it has been a period of great strains and stresses and he had, perforce, to work within certain limitations. True to his policy, he released Sheikh Abdullah from long incarceration. He brought about further integration of the State with the Union and also got changed his nomenclature from that of the Prime Minister to the Chief Minister. But when in pursuance of this policy, Mr Sadiq sought to convert the National Conference itself into the State Unit of the Indian National Congress on January 26, 1965, it extremely upset the Sheikh who embarked upon a movement called "Tarak-i-Mawalat" aiming at the social boycott of the Congressmen in the Valley. The movement fizzled out but left behind traces of bitterness. Meanwhile Sheikh Abdullah had left for Haj pilgrimage which proved more political than religious. He happened to meet among others, Chinese Premier chou-En-Lai abroad and was arrested, following a great hue and cry all over the country, as soon as he landed at Palam Airport New Delhi May 9, 1965. Within less than three months later, Pakistan sent thousands of armed infiltrators into the State and a full-fledged Indo-Pak war ensued followed by an unusual drought.

That Chief Minister Sadiq should have braved all this and survived is, indeed, a matter of no mean achievement. Notwithstanding the doubtful support of a legislature which had refused to elect him as its leader when Bakshi Ghulam Mohd was succeeded by Khwaja Shamsuddin, Mr Sadiq has been able to lay the foundation of an institutionalised administration which had become highly personalized in the hands of his predecessors. But his regime has not been without its failing of its own, either. There have been a few cases, for example, when the press could have been treated more sympathetically. Those hit hard on their part, could also, perhaps, be more responsible. It is hoped that after the general election, Mr Sadiq assured of the loyalty of the Congressmen of his choice in the State Legislature, will be in much better position to translate his pious wishes into action.

# CHAPTER 17

# A Publicist as a Public Man

Life need not be, as perhaps it cannot be divided into water-tight compartments. True, as a reporter it has always been my endeavour to avoid what may be called taking a partisan view. But as a journalist who founded and edited the first newspaper in Jammu and Kashmir, I have my own ideas. These ideas have inevitably landed me in various sphere of public activity at important occasions. Yet my such sojourns have never gone beyond the limits where I have felt I would not be doing justice to my role as conscientious publicist.

**Pro-Congress Activity**

The Ranbir took birth in a climate which was very different from what it is today when we are a free nation committed to such ideals as secularism, democracy and socialism. There was in Jammu and Kashmir little organised political activity as such at that time. The fountain head of all justice was the Maharaja who was also the Chief executive as well as the Commander-in-Chief of the State Forces. Nevertheless, his dependence on British imperialism, was a hard fact. There was a popular saying that the people in the Princely India suffered from double slavery. Mahatma Gandhi was being only realistic when he laid down the strategy that the Indian States were not to be associated with the Congress struggle for freedom that was being launched throughout the British India. This, however, did not constitute any bar to the people in the Indian States themselves making independent efforts to assert their democratic rights.

The Dogra Sadar Sabha (DSS) was the solitary political body in the State during those days. Founded jointly by two lawyers Lala Hans Raj Mahajan and Sahibzada Hazarat Shah, with the good wishes of Maharaja Pratap Singh and Raja Amar Singh, father of Maharaja Hari Singh, in 1905, the DSS provided a common platform to various people belonging to various faiths and regions in Jammu and Kashmir. Under the impact of events in the British India, it began growing into a mass organisation but when the Ranbir was banned in 1931, the DSS was also declared unlawful. It had actually sought affiliation with the Indian National Congress which was, of course, refused. I was an active associate of the DSS all those years and also worked as its General Secretary for a long time.

## All India States' Peoples" Conference

In December 1926, I visited Cawnpore, accompanied by my wife and two children, Om aged nearly five and Suraj aged about three. There I had to play my humble role in getting Pandit Shanker Lal Kaul elected as President of the All-India States' People's Conference whose session was held along with that of the Indian National Congress under the Presidentship of Nightingale of India Mrs Sarojini Naidu. Mr Kaul in the course of his presidential address stressed that the rulers of the Indian States should avoid playing the role of 'little tsars in their kingdoms.'

Mr Kaul was a noble soul. A perfect gentleman he was rather a misfit in his surroundings. He had resigned from the post of Assistant Secretary in the Government of Jammu and Kashmir State in 1925 and had settled in plains. He was a regular subscriber of the Ranbir. He once wrote to me: "Your high character has captivated my heart. We want in Kashmir men, who have honour, who will not lie, who will dare to differ with their friends and agree with their enemies if necessary and with whom patriotism is not mere love of excitement and clamour, men who say the right word, the true word at all times."

Forced by circumstances Mr Kaul later rejoined Government service and retired as the State Publicity Chief. He passed away on September 1, 1952.

## Battle of ballot

On October 17, 1934, Maharaja Hari Singh issued a 700-word proclamation establishing for the first time a Legislative Assembly called Praja Sabha which was more nominated than elected – and that too, on the basis of a restricted and communal franchise. As one who had been persistently insisting on the need for a domestic Legislature in the State, many friends wanted me to contest my home constituency which covered the entire district of Jammu. My rival was Chaudhary Chattar Singh, a former Governor of Jammu Province, who was closely related to the Royal family. He was an affectionate gentleman but belonged the camp of vested interests who were always apprehensive that an Assembly would adversely affect the royal prerogatives. I fought the battle and lost it in an atmosphere surcharged with casteism in its crudest form.

Sheikh Abdullah and his right-hand man at the moment, Pandit Prem Nath Bazaz, in a joint letter dated September 1, 1934, expressing sorrow over my electoral defeat wrote me: "It is generally those selfless workers who make the supreme sacrifices for any cause from the beginning that meet with this fate. You can, however, rely on the experience of your predecessors in the path that the ultimate success is yours and the most earnest efforts you put in, the more failures you face the more shall be the sweetness of the final result."

The daily Milap of Lahore on October 3, 1934, editorially wrote: "Lala Mulk Raj Saraf has fought the election battle with very clean hands. If the atmosphere had not been polluted by bringing in such questions as Mahajan, Rajput, agriculturist, non-agriculturist etc. his success was a certainty. The creation of such vicious atmosphere is extremely detrimental to the Hindus of Jammu and Kashmir and the very first loss that they have suffered thereby is that they have been deprived of their representation in the Assembly by a competent person like Lala Mulk Raj Saraf."

**Decision by lot**

The four-yearly election for the second Praja Sabha was scheduled to be held in May, 1938. I was, again, among the six contestants in the field for the Jammu District (Hindu) seat. There were besides myself, Lala Hans Raj Mahajan Vakil, Pandit Prem Nath Dogra, Brigadier Onkar Singh, Chaudhri Lachchman Singh Charak and Thakur Qandhara Singh, formerly Manager Kashmir State Property in Lahore.

As the atmosphere was somewhat charged with communal tension and caste bickering, it was thought advisable to avoid heat and dust of a contest and have resort to lottery. All agreed. After the scrutiny was over, lots were drawn. The luck favoured the young Charak whose father Chaudhri Chattar Singh had defeated me in 1934 election.

**Towards Regional Harmony**

In 1930's times seemed to be moving rather very fast in the State as well as all over the world. Sheikh Abdullah who was a student when the Ranbir started publication had appeared on the scene as a popular Kashmiri leader with the support of a band of intelligent young men. They carried on their activities under the name of Muslim Conference. But there was little communal about their general outlook. With their emergence, the Dogra Sadar Sabha began to lose its influence with the Kashmiri-speaking gentry. I directed my efforts to bringing the Valley and the DSS closer so as to promote harmony between the two regions at the popular level.

In June 1935, I was deputed by the Dogra Sadar Sabha to meet Prime Minister Colvin in Srinagar in connection with certain grievances of the public particularly relating to the working of two commissions set up by the Government to re-examine the State subject certificates. The Sabha had also authorised me to seek active cooperation of Kashmir leaders in this connection. Accordingly, I held consultations with several friends in Srinagar and a deputation was ultimately arranged.

Col. Colvin was much impressed with what the deputationists had to lay before him. He lost no time in sending a written reply to the deputationists. The very next day after consulting his colleagues in the State Council, Col. Colvin issued a comprehensive order. The first part of the order read: "A deputation consisting Pandit Jia Lal Kilam, Lala Mulk Raj Saraf, Khwaja Ghulam Mohammad Sadiq, Sheikh Mohammad Abdullah and Sardar Kanahyia Singh waited on the Prime Minister on June 27, 1935, in regard to the question of State-subject certificates to examine which two commissions have been set up, one in Srinagar and one in Jammu. They presented a typed memorial and the Prime Minister promised to answer the various points raised in the memorial after consultation with his colleagues. He has now consulted them and decided to convey the following information and decision of Government on the different points raised in the memorial."

And the last para of the order said: "It is hoped that the decision of Government as detailed above will convince all State-subjects that the Government has full sympathy with the aim of making the work of the two commissions real and lasting and that there are only few points of detail on which the Government are not able to agree with the deputation as they involve principles which every Government must affirm,"

**Muslim Conference becomes National Conference**

Ultimately, the Dogra Sadar Sabha could not keep pace with the times. It gradually became a handmaid of reactionary and feudal elements who were incapable of seeing beyond their nose. Sheikh Abdullah and his colleagues on the other hand, were able to organise themselves into a force to be reckoned with. They were also realistic to develop contacts with non-Muslim intelligentsia. At my request the Sheikh spoke from the platform of the DSS once or twice mainly laying emphasis on the Hindu-Muslim unity. Eventually the Sheikh group was itself good enough to think of abandoning their communal label. On June 11, 1939, at a special session of the Muslim Conference held in Mujahid Manzil Srinagar under the presidentship of Khwaja Ghulam Mohammad Sadiq, the resolution seeking the transformation of Muslim Conference into National Conference, was adopted with only three out of about 200 delegates, dissenting. I was in the company of Sardar Budh Singh and Pandit Jia Lal Kilam, Sham Lal Saraf, Prem Nath Bazaz and Kashyap Bandhu as special invitees. We participated in the deliberations when the red plough flag was unanimously adopted as the National Conference flag. Soon after, the first plenary session of the National Conference held at Anantnag affirmed it. I, however, politely declined Sheikh Abdullah's offer to become a member of the first executive of the National Conference as it would have seriously interfered with my work as a journalist. Asked by the Sheikh to suggest another name, I proposed that of Lala Girdhari Lal Anand, a prominent public man of Jammu, who was included in the executive.

**National Conference Inducted in Jammu**

Sheikh Abdullah on his visits to Jammu invariably came to my office where he would spend long hours in developing contacts with prominent local people. Our mutual association was duly noticed by the Hindu communalists. Once when at a public meeting held at Talab Khatikan under the presidentship of Choudhari Ghulam Abbas I spoke of the Sheikh as a great nationalist, I was accused by the Jammu Hindu press of making 'insolent outburst, and also jeeringly dubbed as 'a would-be candidate for a would-be ministership in the would-be Abdullah ministry.'

On November 17, 1940, the foundation of the National Conference was laid in my office. The meeting was presided over by Sardar Budh Singh and attended among others by Sheikh Abdullah, Maulana Masoodi, Sardar Mohinder Singh, Chaudhri Mohammad Shafi, Lala Girdhari Lal Anand, Shri Dina Nath Saraf, Pandit Trilochan Dutt, Mr K.D. Uppal, Shri Gopal Das Dhawan, Shri Balram Bhasin, Lala Hari Chand Chadda, Lala Amar Nath Talwar and Om Saraf, then a student leader.

At one time the Prime Minister, Sir Gopalaswamy Ayyangar had reasons to be much offended with the conduct of the affairs by the National Conference High Command. The National Conference leaders, it appeared could not then for certain reasons, afford to incur displeasure of the Prime Minister and very much wished to have the relation with him normalised. They asked me to intervene in the matter. When I met the Prime Minister, I found his attitude very stiff and uncompromising. "Mr Saraf, you are at liberty to talk to me on any public matter whatsoever but please do not talk to me about these leaders: their behaviour is disgusting" he told me, turning the palm of his right hand across his cheeks as was his wont. It was only after the lapse of some time that the Prime Minister was found in a more chastened and receptive mood to listen to what leaders had got to say. The same Prime Minister and the same National Conference High Command, however, became nearer, if not the nearest, to each other towards the end of the Ayyanger regime in the State so much so that Shri Ayyangar successfully resisted the pressure put on him by the Political Department of Government of India to arrest Sheikh Abdullah during 'Quit India' movement. In the years to come the Sheikh was the Deputy leader of the Indian delegation headed by Shri Ayyangar which went to United Nations to argue Indian complaint of Pakistani aggression on Kashmir.

## 'Quit Kashmir Movement'

With his emergence as energetic nationalist leader it did not take Sheikh Abdullah long to establish cordial relations with the Congress leaders in the British India. In the middle of February 1939, I accompanied the Sheikh to the Ludhiana session of the All-India States' People's Conference held under the presidentship of Pandit Jawahar Lal Nehru who, unlike Gandhiji, believed in actively helping the people in Princely India in hastily getting rid of their feudal regimes. Both of us along with a few other local friends also attended Udaipur session of the AISPC which was again presided over by Mr Nehru in 1945. By then the Sheikh had become an all-India figure. The Udaipur conference greatly added to the popularity and stature of the Sheikh. After the session was over, he accompanied by Sardar Budh Singh, Pandit Sham Lal Saraf and myself toured several parts of Rajasthan.

From Rajasthan Sheikh Abdullah went to Bombay where Maharaja Hari Singh was also staying. There the Sheikh wrote a letter to the Maharaja seeking an interview with him. The reply that the Sheikh got was indeed unfortunate. He was curtly told that a request for interview with the Maharaja could only come through his Prime Minister, Mr R.C. Kak, who was then in Jammu. This greatly disappointed the Sheikh who felt humiliated. No wonder if the foundation of the 'Quit Kashmir' agitation that was later on started by the Sheikh was the result of such frustration. Mr Asaf Ali who defended the Sheikh in the court, described 'Quit Kashmir' as a cry of despair otherwise as he put it "this slogan had no significance other than the establishment of a sound constitutional relationship between a constitutional monarch and the people from whom he should derive his title and power."

## Some other Activities

I have also been associated with various social and other activities. Briefly recollecting, I was elected the President of the three-day sixteenth annual session of All India Mahajan Conference held at Shakargarh, now in Pakistan, in October 1931; made the honorary Joint Secretary of the central committee of the Jammu and Kashmir Bank in 1931; presided over the fourth Northern India Adult Education Conference in Srinagar in August 1943); worked with Shrimati Rameshwar Nehru to collect Kasturba Memorial Fund in the State; was elected President of the Harijan Conference in Khuiratta, Mirpur, now in Pak-occupied Kashmir; led the seven-man delegation on behalf of the Dogri Sanstha Jammu to participate in the first All India Cultural Conference held in Red Fort, Delhi, in March 1952.

*After the Ludhiana Session of the All India States' People's Conference,*
*held in the middle of February 1939, was over, the leading delegates*
*from Jammu and Kashmir were entertained in Lahore at an 'At Home' by an*
*esteemed friend of the author, Shri Tek Chand Dhingra who was then a member*
*of the North West Frontier Province Assembly and was also working as the*
*General Manager of the Daily Pratap, Lahore.*
*(From Right to Left)*
*Kh. G.M. Sadiq, Shri Tek Chand Dhingra, Sheikh Mohammad Abdullah,*
*Shri Sewak Rama Basar, Pt. Prem Nath Bazaz, Pt. Prem Nath Dhar, the*
*Author, Ch. Gian Chand Sadabarti, Maulana Mohd. Sayeed Massoodi,*
*Mr. Waqar Ambalvi, Editor Ehsan, Lahore, and Mr. Ghulam*
*Mohd Jeweller, who became a Minister in "Azad Kashmir Government".*

I have always happily found myself in the midst of ever-enlarging circle of
acquaintances at home and abroad. Such contacts sometimes lead to exchange
of letters. Such correspondence is at once entertaining as well as educative.
I cannot judge the worth of my letters written to others, but I have come, in
the course of time, to possess many invaluable letters from numerous friends

revealing one or the other aspect of a situation or a personality. A few of these letters have been referred to elsewhere. The following extract from an important letter which an American friend sent to me in March 1929 may be read with interest. "I still think of the splendid time I had in Jammu and of your splendid hospitality. I am often with all of you in spirit. I want to help India as far as I can. Please translate the enclosure, publish it in the Ranbir and send me a copy. Will you? If you could smuggle the letter or your Hindustani recast through a reliable Peshawar friend to Kabul, Herat and Kandhar, that it may appear in an Afghan translation in the paper over there, I think, it would be serviceable to the Indian cause. Most people here believe that the Afghan resolution was secretly manipulated by the British Government: such a progressive and independent ruler as the Amir Amanullah might influence, to England's disadvantage, the Maharaja of Kashmir. I am busy lecturing, writing and broadcasting. If India wants me, I am at her beck and call".

**Love for Travel**

In the end I may also take my readers into confidence above another aspect of my life. I love travelling which has benefitted me both as a journalist and otherwise. I am perhaps the most widely travelled journalist in Jammu and Kashmir. My travels made me an eyewitness of many historical occasions. I was eyewitness to Lala Lajpat Rai receiving his share of lethal blows at Lahore on March 10, 1928 (to which, alas, he ultimately succumbed) when Mr Sandres, the European Assistant Superintendent Of Police, had ordered lathi charge on the huge crowd demonstrating against the all-white 7-member Simon Reforms Commission which included Mr Atlee who later became Prime Minister of Great Britain. It was on the same fateful evening that a mammoth public meeting was held outside the Mori Gate Lahore where Lala ji made the prophetic utterance: 'Every blow aimed at me will prove a last nail in the coffin of the British Empire.'

I participated in the Lahore session of the Indian National Congress in December 1929 when it pledged itself, under Pandit Jawahar Lal Nehru's leadership, to the attainment of complete national independence. I was present at the Srinagar special session of the Muslim Conference in June 1939 when it converted itself into the National Conference. In August 1945 I participated in the historical Sopore Session of the National Conference when in the presence of Pandit Jawahar Lal Nehru, Khan Abdul Gaffar Khan (Frontier Gandhi) and Khan Abdul Samad Khan (Baluchi Gandhi), it adopted the socio-economic plan of 'New Kashmir' as its ultimate objective. I also attended the Lahore session of the All-India Muslim League as a pressman when in July 1944 it declared Pakistan to be its goal.

In May 1945, in consultation with the great educationist Mr K.G. Saiyidain who was the State's Director of Education, I journeyed to Hyderabad to study the working of Osmania University. This visit reinforced me in my view to get established a university in my own State. I continued my efforts for the purpose which was achieved only in 1948. I had the good fortune of flying to Delhi to take part in Gandhiji's funeral and pay my last homage to the father of the Nation on January 31, 1948. The solemn occasion moved me – as everyone else – to the depth of my heart and was also reminiscent of the never-to-be forgotten days when I used to sit at Gandhiji's feet, first at the prayer hours at the Lahore residence of Sarla Devi Chaudharani, wife of Shri Rambhuj Dutt and then after partition at the Birla House, New Delhi.

I was thrilled to see the inauguration by Sheikh Abdullah of Constituent Assembly of Jammu and Kashmir in Srinagar in November 1951. I was also present, 8 years later, in the Court of Special Magistrate, when the Sheikh was made an accused in what is known as the Kashmir Conspiracy case.

As indicated earlier I attended the First World Congress of Journalists at Helsinki (Finland) and later had opportunity to visit some other foreign lands. I was privileged to attend the momentous Bombay session of the Indian Federation of Working Journalists inaugurated by Pandit Jawahar Lal Nehru in December 1963.

*With Prime Minister Jawaharlal Nehru, as member of*
*the Executive of the Indian Federation of Working Journalists,*
*New Delhi (February 18, 1964)*

It has been always my effort to be in Delhi on Republic Day celebrations and occasional visits there by the leading men of the world such as Queen Elizabeth, President Eisenhower, Mr Khrushchev and Mr Bulganin.

I have also not my fondness of travel on foot which I acquired in my early days when I had often to cover 25 miles distance between my hometown Samba and the capital city of Jammu, not always without a headload. This has indeed enabled me to keep, in all humility, my head erect in every sense of the word.

# CHAPTER 18

# Golden Jubilee

I completed my seventy second year on April 8, 1966 running my fiftieth year as a journalist. The Sach, a popular local Urdu Weekly which had been founded by a great freedom fighter Raja Mohammad Akbar Khan, in 1930's, has been serialising my autobiography for more than two years now. Its editor Master Roshan Lal thought of celebrating the occasion by throwing open 'At home'.

Among those who attended the function were Ministers Trilochan Dutt, Mohammad Ayub Khan, Pir Gias-ud-Din and A.M. Tariq, State Jana Sangh Chief Prem Nath Dogra and his General Secretary Rishi Kumar Koushal, PSP Chief Dhan Raj Bhagotra, Wazir Ganga Ram former Home Minister, Brigadier Ghansar Singh, ex-Governor Gilgit, Shri Milkhi Ram, President Harijan Mandal, Shri R.N. Chowdhry, President Chamber of Commerce, Jammu, besides many other prominent citizens including, of course, all brother journalists.

In addition to the host, several others spoke on the occasion to praise my services in the cause of journalism. Minister Tariq recalled how he began his career with the Rattan. He said he could barely believe that I was 72. Offering me a bouquet Pandit Baldev Prasad Sharma, Director, Radio Kashmir, Jammu stated he was proud to claim that he had his earliest lessons in journalism at my hands. Pandit Prem Nath Dogra with whom I have had many occasions to differ during the course of long years of our association as publicmen, expressed his admiration for what he called my perfect sincerity of the purpose. Shri D.C. Prashant of P.T.I. remembered the days when the Ranbir played an important role on several crucial occasions in the history of the State. Shi Ved Bhasin, Editor the Kashmir Times, and Chaudhry Gian Chand too had a good word for my services in the cause of the people both as a publicist and a publicman.

*The Author at 72 with his sons Left to Right (Sitting) Om,*
*The Author, Suraj (Standing) Ved, Prem, Sat*

*In the hey-day of "Hindi-Chini Bhai Bhai" with the Chinese Prime Minister Chou-en-Lai in Peking (July 1956)*

*Reception by North Korean Prime Minister Kim iL Sung (middle) in Pyongyang, Capital of North Korea (July 25, 1956)*

*At Lenin Mausoleum, Red Square, Moscow (June 20, 1956)*

*On a seashore in Helsinki wearing badges of the International*
*Organisation of Journalists (June 12, 1956)*

*With Rashtrapati Dr. Rajendra Prasad, as leader of the Dogra Sanstha Delegation which participated in the All India Cultural Conference (March 17 and 18, 1951) and displayed masterpieces of Dogra School of Paintings in Dewan-e-Khas, Red Fort, Delhi. The photograph was taken at a reception held in Rashtrapati Bhawan (March 19, 1951)*

Overwhelmed by such tributes, I thanked the host and others who had rather profoundly expressed their regard and affection for me. I assured them of my continued public service through journalism without fear or favour.

Many newspapers in and outside the State widely publicised the Golden Jubilee celebrations. The Blitz, Bombay, published a story with my picture speaking of "handsome tributes paid to the veteran journalist". The Kashmir Times wrote about "many 'firsts' to his credit. Besides the Ranbir, he started the first children's magazine, the Rattan; set up the first printing press, attended the first world journalists meet at Helsinki; is the first State journalist who has widely travelled all over Europe, USSR and China; presided over the first All Jammu and Kashmir Newspapers' Conference; and continues to be the first President of the Jammu and Kashmir Union of Working Journalists besides being a member of the Executive of All India Federation of Working Journalists". The Milap, New Delhi, in a feature described me as "the father of journalism in Jammu and Kashmir" and spoke of my honest discharge of duty as a journalist."

I was the recipient of numerous messages of felicitations and greetings from the friends so well-known in the world of journalism. Shri P.P. Singh, Head of Department of Punjab University, wrote: "You have done pioneering work in the field of journalism in your State and served the Fourth Estate with the best in you. May you hit a century and more and more continue to serve the profession with zeal and fervour. It was a pleasure travelling with you from here to Finland, Russia, China and back home. I treasure the memories of happy times spent in your good company".

Shri Virendra, Chief Editor of the daily Pratap, said, "May I congratulate you heartily on this occasion? It is indeed very gratifying to see a fellow journalist securing such a great success in his life and profession. You have kept the torch of freedom of expression always burning."

Rana Jang Bahadur Singh, a former Editor of the Tribune and the Times of India stated: "Your many-sided contribution to the development of journalism in Jammu and Kashmir covering a considerable long period is tremendous. Not many journalists like you are left in our midst. I pay my humble tributes to you and your valuable work and wish you many a happy return of your birthday. I recall today with pleasure and pride my long and close association with you in the professional work and activities from Lahore to Helsinki and onward – we have travelled a memorable distance together."

Shri Balraj Puri, PSP leader, wired from New Delhi his "felicitations on golden jubilee of an eventful and inspiring career." Shri D.C. Sharma Member Parliament, wrote "we all feel proud of what you have done in educating public opinion in Jammu and Kashmir". And so did many others.

By the grace of God and the good wishes of a large number of friends all over the country, I am fit even today at 73, to carry out the mission of my life through pen, I may not be considered worldly-wise enough to have created a property in its crude form but I have complete satisfaction in having uphold certain values of life at any rate and helping a band of youngmen including my sons to get initiated in the noble profession of journalism and its allied spheres as responsible people ever prepared to work and to suffer, if need be, as conscientious journalists.

# Appendix I



*The statement issued on September 11, 1956, from Srinagar:*

Ever since my return from the tour of some of the European and Asian countries like France, Finland, Russia, China, Korea, Hong-Kong etc. after participating in the First World Congress of Journalists at Helsinki in June 1956, friends have been asking me to give detailed narration of what I saw in these countries. Several articles embodying my impressions of the tour have already appeared in various local newspapers as the Khidmat, the Martand, the Jyoti, the Sach, the Haqiqat and the Kashmir Times.

Here are in a summarized form, some of the important impressions that I have had during my recent foreign tour:

**As a Journalist:** It was clear like broad-day light that the journalists, as ears and eyes of the world, are determined as never before to make their contribution to international peace and progress of mankind as a whole.

**As a Citizen of the World:** The World is rapidly becoming one; communal, regional and even national barriers are withering away in face of new social values and all-round developmental activities – whether it is in already much-advanced Russia or war-ridden Korea.

**As an Indian:** There is a growing respect for India and for her great Prime Minister Pandit Jawahar Lal Nehru. I also noticed particular admiration in Korea, for Indian Army and its humane, valiant officers and disciplined soldiers.

**As a Jammu and Kashmir Citizen:** I found that everywhere people were interested in Kashmir not only as a lovely beauty spot, but also as a first-rate political problem. We may expect many more visitors before long from the East European countries including Russia where Kashmir's continued association with India is widely appreciated in the cause of world peace.

My travels have convinced me that journalists are necessary as, if not more than, teachers, technicians and politicians for the achievement of our ideal of "New Kashmir" here. Let journalism become a mission of life with some of our young men and we will see how through proper training and experience they are capable of making a vital contribution to the mighty endeavour of our national reconstruction.

I have also to make a concrete suggestion for the immediate consideration of all concerned and, that is, that the State journalists' delegations should be deputed on visits to South, East Asia and Middle East Regions. These our neighbours, are going to play an important role in the World Affairs in the near future and it will be to our mutual advantage if we take steps sooner the better, to let them have a complete picture of the actual state of affairs in Jammu and Kashmir.

# Appendix II

*The Welcome Address on behalf of the Jammu Journalists Association read out by its General Secretary Shri D.C. Prashant on August 17, 1956.*

----------

Respected Lala Sahib,

We, the members of the Journalists' Association, are assembled here today to say our welcome to you on the eve of your back-home from the European and Asian tour. We take the opportunity of expressing the deep gratitude we owe you for your splendid work in the field of journalism in the State.

## Pioneer of Journalism

You are pioneer of journalism in the State. You started your weekly "Ranbir" under several odds of the time and when journalism was unknown to the people here. Your paper the "Ranbir", reached the zenith of its glory in a short period of its impartial, unbiased and nationalist outlook. It is unfortunate that the Paper has ceased to exist but its cherished memory has made a permanent abode in the people's hearts. Your writings for the outside papers can be described as "from a neutral observer". By electing you the President of the Journalists' Association we have brought a right person in the right place.

You have travelled several countries of the world and your knowledge and experience which, as we hope, would benefit others also. And with refreshed energy you will resume your work you love so much.

We earnestly request you to accept this humble token of our great love and respect for you and we welcome you being again amidst us. With best wishes for your health, happiness and prosperity.

# Appendix III



**PRESIDENTIAL ADDRESS**

*At the fourth Northern India Adult Education Conference, Srinagar on August 30, 1943.*

----------

Adult education has been one of the basic problems even in advanced countries like England and America. Universities, industrial concerns, philanthropic associations have started adult education centres where special courses are arranged for improving the efficiency of the technical and industrial workers and for imparting and developing the artistic, the literary and the recreational side of the life of the citizens. It is indeed tragic to contemplate that we in India are still engaged on the preliminary task of imparting mere literacy. And even here in the Jammu and Kashmir State we are handicapped in many ways. Our system of administration has its short-comings and is not yet what we desire it to be. Our resources are limited, our sense of social responsibility is not yet fully developed and our realisation of our duties towards our less fortunate neighbours is not what it ought to be. A national Scheme of Adult Education in the State should, to my mind, comprise not only a frontal attack on the appalling illiteracy of about 36 lakhs of people of both sexes but also an organisation on a mass scale of facilities for providing education on health and hygiene, the economic regeneration, the industrial expansion and above all the political awakening. The present world war of an all-embracing character has demonstrated that even for training the soldiers in the art of killing each other, a high standard of physical resistance and mental alertness is absolutely necessary. And not only that but also an intelligent understanding of why wars are fought and what the ideologies inspiring the belligerents are. These techniques, skills and attitudes are imparted to the soldiers in the numerous training centres that have been organised everywhere. If those engaged on murdering each other in the name of national interests or it may be to save humanity, require such intensive education, how much more is required for a citizen who is expected not to kill but to improve the lot of his fellow countrymen.

I think that the day is not very distant when this type of Adult Education will come into vogue in our country. We shall have for many years yet to concentrate on the humbler and less spectacular task of providing the general mass of people with mere tools of learning, that is, imparting them the skill to read and understand the printed page or to write out their ideas for communication to others. Even this humble task will require thousands of selfless workers imbued with the zeal of patriots who will carry this message of literacy to every hearth and home in this land.

Recently there has grown up a body of opinions which seems to have no faith in the scheme of adult education as pursued at present in our State. The impression has been let out that the *bona fides* of the Education department are not honest and that the Scheme has been conceived either as an eyewash or as pro-Government propaganda. I am not here very much concerned in either condemning or defending the intentions and activities of the Education Department in this behalf. But I am strongly of the view that the intelligent public should never fail to recognize and emphasize the place of adult education in the national reconstruction of the country in all its phases and should exploit even pro-Government propaganda if thereby it can advance the true interests of the masses. It is only on this ground that I deplore the recent ill-conceived and hasty orders of His Highness's Government suspending funds that was originally budgeted for the adult education scheme. We may have differences of opinion on the way the funds should have been utilized but the withdrawal of the financial aid by the Government at the present juncture is an act on which the Government cannot congratulate themselves. A small sum of forty thousand rupees a year on a national building scheme like this should not have been grudged by a Government claiming to be progressive in its outlook and solicitous of the educational and social advancement of the people. I can only hope that those in power will realise, if they have not already done so, the short-sightedness of their decisions and restore, if not augment, the funds for the activity. I know that there are other difficulties also. To provide educational facilities in a country where means of communication are so very difficult, where the economic standard is so low and where ignorance is so deep-rooted, is, by no means, an easy task. But these difficulties and obstacles have got to be overcome. Those who feel with me that the Adult Education is a significant need of times should not feel discouraged by the present indifferent attitude of the Government. They should rather take it up as a challenge to their sense of self-respect and patriotism and intensify by all means at their disposal the movement for education of the adult. The responsibility on public organisations is particularly imperative and they can justify their existence as true well-wishers of the masses, in the measure in which they throw themselves whole-heartedly into this work of national reconstruction. Young men, especially college and school students should be organised in this crusade against ignorance, and they should realise that their own education is only a trust which they should utilise in the service of others.

I wish to make one thing clear. Adult education is not an activity that can be taken up in a light mood or with a view to gain goodwill of those whose favours the workers are anxious to earn. Adult education, apart from raising the civic standard of the people and training them, both men and women, for better living, is a potent weapon in a country like India which is on the threshold of great social and political advancement. Adult education is a serious business which will claim the whole of earnestness, time, intelligence and patriotism of those engaged in it. But the return to the worker would be much simpler than what he contributes. He will come in contact with and learn at first hand the conditions of life of what is vulgarly but very expressively called the underdog and if he is endowed with a heart that feels, he will dedicate his all to ameliorate the lot of this large class of people. When that day dawns the future of the masses and hence of humanity will be less despondent than it is today.

If the State Government were so sympathetic as our August Ruler is for the welfare of the people, they should not find it difficult to draw up a plan in cooperation with public, designed not only to impart literacy but also to provide opportunity for an all-round education for the entire adult population of the State. And this plan can very well be spread over a reasonable period of, say ten or fifteen years. But any scheme must ensure to the poor worker, who is obsessed with the idea of feeding his family, a scale of living wages which will relieve him for coming Adult Education Center and benefitting by the instructions imparted there. This will serve both as an inducement and relief and will give impetus to the movement. The teacher need not necessarily be a school teacher, doing extra work and tired by hard day's toil. All the public bodies and associates who are interested in the social, political and economic welfare of this country should pursue the work once begun in right earnest. Other workers, paid or honorary, may be invited to take up the work. Even the school teacher needs to be vitalised into progressive activity by proper training and sufficient remuneration.

Your organisation composed, as I take it to be, of workers in the cause of Adult Education, should give a lead in organising a workable scheme which can serve as a guide to others who may feel interested in contributing their on mite to the sacred cause of adult education.

It should be a great encouragement to the Conference that its proceedings have been inaugurated by an Educationist of Mr K.G. Saiyidain's position and repute. He has fathered the movement of Adult Education in the State and I have heard from him the other day with satisfaction that the withdrawal of the Government grant is not interpreted as a cessation of the adult Education work so far as his department is concerned. In close cooperation with the Education Department, the publicmen and public organisations should give this movement a fillip and make it as nation-wide as it is right and proper that it should be.

To those present in this House, I strongly appeal in the name of this great country that they would, each one in his or her own place and with the resources at his or her disposal, take active part in the movement to spread adult literacy and hold himself or herself responsible for at least two persons literate every year. Adult Education in India is a dire necessity of time and sooner or later the leaders of the country shall have to devote their full attention to make this movement a great success.

I once again thank you, ladies and gentlemen, for the honour you have done me and the patience with which you have heard me this evening.

# Message

## A Missionary

I have gone through the autobiography of Shri Mulk Raj Saraf with great interest and care. It gives a vivid picture of the struggle which the author had to go through before he reached his goal. It appears from his biography that the author had chief ambition in life to become a successful journalist. He had to meet great hardships and overcome number pf hurdles before he established himself as journalist. He is hard-working, honest and a man of strong convictions. He worked as a missionary regardless of any temptation which came his way. Hese are the qualities which account for his success. Although the book is not an exhaustive chronicle of the Jammu and Kashmir State, yet it depicts the different stages of reforms which took place in the State. It further shows how the author laid the foundation of journalism in the State and how gradually it progressed and reached the present stage. That is why Shri Saraf, the author, has been affectionately known as the father of journalism in Jammu and Kashmir State. People interested in journalism and in the history of our State will find interesting material in this book for their study.

Janaki Nath Wazir
Acting Governor
(Chief Justice Jammu & Kashmir High Court)
Jammu
April 10, 1967

# Message

### High Standards of Moral Rectitude

Reading through this book recall the year of endeavours, of despair, of hopes and of trials which the author's generation faced during the first half of the twentieth century. The author sketches the life of the Ranbir, the first newspaper in Jammu and Kashmir, which he started with meagre help, continued to publish with a liberal outlook, and closed because of official displeasure. The urge which drove him to undertake the venture and the high standard of moral rectitude which he maintained, are typical of the journalists' school to which he belonged. The fact of the Ranbir having been published in an Indian State only shows that the struggle for freedom was catholic and not confined to what was then called British India.

Some of his readers, however, would be disappointed at author's not giving views about why his State, notwithstanding able hands, had not attained the standard of administrative efficiency which some other Indian States reached elsewhere. His comments about the administrative and judicial setup in the State would have been helpful. But whatever the omission the book with its comments on the persons and events will always find a welcome place on the tables of those engaged in comparative study of India as it is today.

M.A. Ansari
Retired Chief /justice, Kerala High Court
Ex-Chairman
Anti-corruption Commission
Jammu and Kashmir State
Jammu
May 12, 1967

# Publisher's Note

## A World Record

The 26-year-old Lala Mulk Raj Saraf started as a reporter with 'Bande Matram' at Lahore early in 1920. He had, though, fallen in love with writing for newspapers around 1916 as a College student. His earliest assignments as reporter included coverage of the Hunter Commission set up by the British Government to inquire into the Jallianwala Bagh massacre by General Dyer. Even as Editor of 'Ranbir' (1924-50) while reporting major events for his own paper, he worked as Correspondent of several prominent national dailies. Reporting attracted his exclusive attention when 'Ranbir' ceased publication. He was representing 'The Hindu', Madras, when he suddenly passed away at the age of 95, which made him the world record holder as an active reporter for 70 years. To have done it in a sensitive region like Jammu and Kashmir in keeping with the best traditions of his noble profession earned him the title of 'Father of Journalism' both at the popular and official levels.

(In some chapters the dates and years mentioned are as per the Indian calendar and retained as in the original autobiography).

-------------------------------------------------------

(Lala Mulk Raj Saraf passed away in Mumbai in February 1989)

# Afterword

My memories of Chachaji, as we lovingly called my great-grandfather, Lala Mulk Raj Saraf, remain vivid and cherished. I remember him as a larger-than-life figure, always surrounded by people seeking his wisdom. His presence commanded both respect and affection. The Padmashri citation proudly displayed in his home was a constant reminder of his immense contributions, but it wasn't until I read his autobiography later in life that I truly understood the depth of his sacrifice and unwavering commitment to journalism.

As a trustee of the JDGD Saraf Trust, which he founded, I feel a deep sense of responsibility in republishing his autobiography to commemorate 100 years of journalism in Jammu and Kashmir (J&K). This book is being reprinted by the Trust to honor his legacy and to share his inspiring journey with new generations. His life is a testament to courage, resilience, and an unflinching dedication to truth – values that are as relevant today as they were a century ago.

In 1924, the first newspaper, Ranbir, was printed in J&K. In today's world of instant news, where information flows effortlessly across the globe, it is easy to take for granted the freedom we have to share our voices. Yet, as Chachaji's journey reveals, the birth of journalism in J&K was anything but easy. For him, starting a newspaper was not just a monumental task; it was an act of defiance, bravery, and persistence against forces that sought to suppress free speech. Today, as we grapple with questions about media freedom, credibility, and the role of journalism in society, his story serves as a powerful reminder that the struggle to uphold the truth is timeless. Chachaji was a man driven by purpose. Orphaned at a young age, he faced challenges that would have discouraged many, yet he remained steadfast in his vision to give J&K a voice. Reading his autobiography filled me with awe at how selfless and determined he was – dedicating his life to a cause bigger than himself. His journey from a penniless youth to an institution builder is a lesson in perseverance, integrity, and purpose.

In republishing his autobiography, I hope to share with today's readers the same awe and inspiration I have felt. This is not just a historical document; it is the story of a man who embodied entrepreneurship in the truest sense of the word. For my great-grandfather, entrepreneurship wasn't about building businesses for profit—it was about challenging the status quo, forging new paths, and using the resources available to create something meaningful for society. His life reminds us that entrepreneurship, in any field, is about vision, action, and persistence. It reminds us of the power of one individual's vision to shape an entire society and inspire us to remain fearless in the pursuit of truth, justice, and purpose.

With deep respect and admiration, the Trustees of the JDGD Saraf Trust present this reprint of the autobiography of the "Father of Journalism" in J&K. May his legacy continue to inspire future generations of journalists, entrepreneurs, and changemakers.

Dr. Sonali Gupta
Jammu
June 2024